Arduino Programming

The Ultimate Guide for Making the Best of Your Arduino Programming Projects

by Damon Parker

© Copyright 2020—All Rights Reserved

herein, either directly or indirectly. The author owns all copyrights not held by the publisher.

The information herein is provided for educational purposes exclusively and is universal. The presentation of the information is without contractual agreement or any kind of warranty assurance.

All trademarks inside this book are for clarifying purposes only and are possessed by the owners themselves, not allied with this document.

Disclaimer

All erudition supplied in this book is specified for educational and academic purposes only. The author is not in any way in charge of any outcomes that emerge from using this book. Constructive efforts have been made to render information that is both precise and effective, but the author is not to be held answerable for the accuracy or use/misuse of this information.

Foreword

I will like to thank you for taking the very first step of trusting me and deciding to purchase/read this life-transforming book. Thanks for investing your time and resources in this product.

I can assure you of precise outcomes if you will diligently follow the specific blueprint I lay bare in the information handbook you are currently checking out. It has transformed lives, and I firmly believe it will equally change your own life too.

All the information I provided in this Do It Yourself piece is easy to absorb and practice.

Table of Contents

INTRODUCTION

Thank you for purchasing this book: Arduino Programming—The Ultimate Beginner's Guide. In this book, we are going to give you a summary of the concepts that you have to understand before you begin Arduino programming. We will explain to you the different components that you should learn about before you delve and go into establishing more intricate programs for different operating systems. The Arduino programming language has many benefits.

Nevertheless, it also has various little elements that can leave you perplexed. Not having the ability to comprehend these aspects can trigger some issues in the future. In this book, we're going to talk about what those aspects are. We are also going to talk about what Arduino is, where it originated from, and all of the essential ideas that you have to understand before you begin programming. Additionally, we'll also teach you how to setup and use the Code Blocks IDE, which will assist you significantly when programming Arduino language. We hope you enjoy this book.

CHAPTER ONE

What Is Arduino Programming?

Arduino is a computer software application and hardware business or community that produces and develops microcontroller packages for robotics as well as other digital gadgets.

The name "Arduino" originates from the name of a bar at Ivrea, Italy, where some of the founders of this project used to meet. Nowadays, this is the most favourite tool of modern-day robotics. Before starting with an Arduino microcontroller, one should know the variety of the Arduinos. Some of entry-level Arduino's are:

- UNO

- LEONARDO

- 101

- ROBOT

- ESPLORA

- MICRO

- NANO

- MINI

- MKR2UNO ADAPTER

- STARTER KIT

- BASIC KIT

- LCD SCREEN

These Arduinos are simple to use, and all set to power one's first robot. These boards are the best to begin discovering and to code your bots through the microcontrollers.

These were about the hardware. Now let's consider the Arduino software. Each of these boards is programmable with the Arduino IDE. This is a cross-platform application written in the programming language Java. C and C++ are also supported in this IDE with special rules. A program written in Arduino IDE is called a sketch. These sketches are conserved as the text files with the file extensions.ino and.pde. A minimal Arduino sketch consists of two functions. They are; setup and loop.

Arduino ROBOT is the very first Arduino on wheels. It consists of two boards, and each of the boards has a microcontroller. That indicates that in ROBOT there is an overall of two microcontrollers. One of them is the motor board, which manages the motors, and the other one is the control panel, which oversees the sensors and chooses the operations. It is also programmable with Arduino IDE. Both the microcontroller boards are based on ATmega32u4, which is a low-power CMOS 8-bit microcontroller based on the AVR enhanced RISC architecture. The ROBOT is similar to LEONARDO.

As a novice in robotics, Arduino is the most valuable tool you'll find. It is an open-source electronic devices platform based upon easy-to-use software and hardware. Arduino boards can check out inputs—light on a sensor, a finger on a button, or a Twitter message—and turn it into an output—triggering a motor, turning on an LED. You can instruct your board on what to do by sending out a set of relevant directions to the on-board microcontroller.

To do so, use the Arduino programming language (created on Wiring) and the Arduino Software (IDE), built for Processing.

Over the years, Arduino has been the brain of countless projects, from daily things to complex scientific instruments. An around the world community of makers—students, hobbyists, artists, developers, and specialists—has collected this open-source platform; their contributions have included a fantastic quantity of accessible knowledge that can be of help to professionals and novices.

Arduino was developed at the Ivrea Interaction Design Institute as an easy tool for quick prototyping, focused on trainees without a background in electronic devices and programming. As quickly as it reached a wider community, the Arduino board started changing to adapt to new requirements and challenges, separating its offer from easy 8-bit boards to products for IoT applications, wearable, 3D printing, and ingrained environments. Most Arduino boards are open-source, empowering users to build them independently and eventually adjust them to their specific needs. The software is also open-source, and it is growing through the contributions of users worldwide.

Why Arduino?

Thanks to its available and straightforward user experience, Arduino has been used in countless jobs and applications. The Arduino software application is easy-to-use for beginners yet versatile enough for advanced users. It runs on Mac, Windows, and Linux.

Educators and trainees use it to construct low expense clinical instruments, to show chemistry and physics principles, or to start with programming and robotics.

Architects and designers construct interactive prototypes; artists and workers use it for installations and to experiment with brand-new musical instruments.

Makers, of course, use it to construct many tasks displayed at the Maker Faire, for instance. Arduino is a crucial tool to find out new things. Anybody; children, hobbyists, artists, developers can start playing just following the step by action directions of a kit or sharing concepts online with other members of the Arduino community.

There are lots of other microcontrollers platforms offered for physical computing. Netmedia's BX-24, Phidgets, Parallax Basic Stamp, MIT's Handyboard, and many others provide comparable functionality. All of these tools take the messy information of microcontroller programming and cover it up in a user-friendly plan. Arduino also simplifies the process of dealing with microcontrollers, but it offers some advantage for teachers, trainees, and interested amateurs over other systems:

- **Inexpensive** – Arduino boards are reasonably cheap compared to other microcontroller platforms. The least pricey version of the Arduino module can be assembled by hand, and even the pre-assembled Arduino modules cost less than $50.

- **Cross-platform** – The Arduino Software (IDE) works on Windows, Macintosh OSX, and Linux operating systems. Most microcontroller systems are restricted to Windows.

- **Easy, transparent programming environment** – The Arduino Software (IDE) is easy-to-use for newbies yet versatile enough to benefit innovative users. For teachers, it is suitably based on the programming environment, so trainees discovering to program because the environment will be quite familiar with the way Arduino IDE works.

- **An Open source and extensible software** – The Arduino software is published as open-source tools available for extension by experienced programmers. The language can be broadened through C++ libraries, and individuals desiring to comprehend the technical information can make the leap from Arduino to the AVR Arduino programming language on which it is based. Likewise, you can add AVR-C code directly to your Arduino programs if you wish.

- **Open Source and Extensible Hardware** – The designs of the Arduino boards are available under the Creative Commons license, and professional circuit designers can create their edition of the platform, expand it, and develop it. Even relatively inexperienced users can construct the breadboard version of the module to understand how it works and save cash.

Arduino – The Most Popular Way to Regulate Robots

There are many ways to manage robots. This book will go over one of the most preferred approaches presently used on the planet, the 'Arduino'. It is very basic. It is just a physical computing platform for performing valuable jobs when interfaced (connected) to a computer. 'Arduino' is an open resource project, which means capable individuals in the robotics area can contribute and also enhance the 'Arduino'.

The advantages of using the 'Arduino' atmosphere is that it is extremely user-friendly. Any person with zero levels of electronics and program skills can now find out to program robotics. Incidentally, when it is said that programs robotics, this means composing a specific amount of codes to the 'microcontroller' of the robot. Keep in mind that the 'microcontroller' acts as the mind for the robot.

Generally, when somebody uses 'Arduino' to control robotics, that implies he or she is making use of the software application called 'Arduino IDE', in which 'IDE' means Integrated Growth Atmosphere. This program has been developed extensively and is at no cost. Simply put, it is free software. To compose codes, one will certainly discover the 'Arduino' language. It is mainly based on the currently well known 'C++ programming language'. If you have shown skills or experience in the past, programming robots making use of 'Arduino' is a wind for you.

'Arduino' is well-known until it is commonly manufactured and in some cases made in some variations by third party suppliers. They have acquired broad spread appeal for the last five years. I think the 'Arduino' is an expanding treasure in the eyes of the world today. Check it out and also see it on your own if you are a robotics fan.

Arduino – A Physical Computing Platform for Robotic Programming

'Arduino', is an open-source physical computing system based on the 'Atmel', 'AVR', 'Atmega' mini controller board. It is also a development atmosphere for writing programming codes or software application for the growth board.

The 'Arduino' can be created to interact with objects, inputs, and for this reason, regulating physical outputs like lights and electric motors can be a stand-alone or talk to the computer system.

Its language is an integration of 'Wiring', a comparable physical computer system, based on the 'Processing' multimedia setting atmosphere. The program codes work as if they were C language. 'Arduino' is selected for its many advantages. One would be its price. The 'Arduino' software application can work greater than one system; Windows, 'Macintosh OSX', and also

Linux (32bit and 64 bit) operating systems. Its straightforward programming atmosphere ('Handling') is precious to both mini controller novices as well as professionals.

Because of its open resource nature as well as the complimentary integrated established environment ('IDE'), it is a preferred selection worldwide. Improvisations of the boards are continually made by knowledgeable circuit designers, under the Creative Commons license.

The 'Arduino IDE' (version 0018) software application operates to create, put together as postcodes to the microcontroller. The connection from the computer system to the mini controller growth board is by 'USB'. Software programs or codes written in the 'IDE' are called sketches in the text editor. It also a beneficial serial display that acts like Hyper Terminal.

Like the C language, it is comparable. The standard framework of the 'Arduino' programming language is essential; it runs in a minimum of two blocks of codes, the void arrangement, and gap loophole. Whereby the last holes continually, like its said name, and also declarations in the agreement just run as soon as confirmations.

A Short Look at the Arduino System

Arduino is an open-source, programmable microcontroller and software based on the ATMega chip. Although the Arduino is developed as a prototyping platform, it can be used in different electronic devices jobs, whether short-term or ingrained.

The Arduino board can be programmed using the Arduino software application.

The phrase structure for this resembles C/C++ and Java.

It is designed for easy use and can be run by anyone, from novices to professionals alike.

As Arduino is an open-source platform, you can get hold of the source code and schematics for it. This means you can delve right into it as you want, even creating your personal Arduino boards.

How Do I Use Arduino?

If you are looking for motivation, you can discover a great variety of tutorials on Arduino Project Hub.

The Getting Started with Arduino guide is accredited under a Creative Commons Attribution-ShareAlike 3.0 license. Code samples in the book are launched into the public domain.

CHAPTER TWO

Introduction to Arduino Programming Language

Like most new projects, when you set out to do programming, you discover yourself surrounded by weird and possibly odd terms, as well as fancied lingo. In this book, we'll examine those terms in addition to present an introduction of the whole programming process. It is extremely most likely that you're excited to begin writing codes, and you may have currently viewed a later chapter in this book. It is essential to know a few basic terms and programming principles.

History of Arduino Programming Language

Back in 1972, a computer scientist at AT&T's Bell Laboratories started to develop some programs he required for his use.

Dennis Ritchie began developing what has progressed into the Arduino programming language.

He was trying to make computing as easy as possible. Dennis Ritchie realized that the then-current assembly language was much intricate. They attempted to reverse this trend by constructing an easy programming language on a minicomputer. What Dennis Ritchie wished to preserve was not only an efficient computer system programming language in which to produce programs, but also a computer system programming language which programming community could form a fellowship. They knew, based on previous experiences that the real nature of joint computing as provided by time-shared, remote accessed systems is not merely to get computer system code into a terminal but to encourage post programming communication. The Arduino Programming language is a primary function and structured programming language.

It is also called a procedural oriented programming language that is not mainly designed for particular application areas. However, it was well matched for business and scientific applications. It has different features like control structures, looping statements, and micros needed for applications. The Arduino programming language has the following features:

- Portability

- Flexibility

- Effectiveness and efficiency

- Reliability

- Interactivity

What Is Programming?

Programming is where you develop a software application. The software manages hardware, which is the visible part of an electronic gadget such as a computer system, phone, tablet, gaming console, micro-controller, or some other device. Those instructions take the type of programming language. For this book, that language is the Arduino programming language, which was developed back in the early 1970s. It is ancient. In reality, over, time the Arduino programming language has been thought as the Latin of programming languages.

Unlike Latin, Arduino programming is still alive. Great deals of Arduino Programming still goes on despite the recent and fancier programming languages happening. Like Latin, Arduino is the structure on which many other programming languages are constructed. You can quickly discover other languages if you understand Arduino. In a later chapter, we will discuss the programming language's syntax and different rules. For now, know that the code you write is called source code.

What Is a Source Code?

Source code is a plain text file that includes the programming language, all formatted and pretty, as well as written excellently. In Arduino, the file is saved with a.c filename extension. To produce source code, you use a full-screen editor. Any full-screen editor can do, although some editors give handy features like colour coding, line numbers, syntax monitoring, and other tools. The source code is then put together into object code. The program that produces the item code is called a compiler. The traditional name of the Arduino language compiler is CC, which represents C compiler. The compiler reads the source code file and creates an object code file. Object code files have a.o filename extension, and they use the same filename as the initial source code file.

The next action is called Linking. It is frequently forgotten because modern-day compilers link and put together, but connecting is actually a different action. The linker takes the item code file and combines it with Arduino language libraries. The libraries are the workhorse of the language. They consist of routines and functions that manage every gadget you are programming.

If all goes well, the end result is a program file. You can then check run the program to ensure that it works the way you want it. And if not, you start the cycle all over again: modify, compile and connect, or "develop," and evaluate run.

All these tools—the editor, compiler, linker, all came from the command terminal or prompt. You can still discover them there also. Because it is fast, programmers do a lot of coding at the command timely. Commonly, use an IDE, or Integrated Development Environment.

What Is an IDE?

An IDE, or Integrated Development Environment, combines the tools for editing, putting together, connecting, and running. It also includes tools for debugging, producing intricate programs, other functions, and visual tools. Above all, is the humble command line compiler and linker. The process is the same: edit, compile and connect, run. You are going to do many re-working and repeating before you get things right. Fortunately, that is all the tools you need to start your programming journey for free on the internet. The problem being that you need to find the right tools and install them properly.

This is not an issue for you here because in this book, we'll show you how it is done. You will see how to discover a great IDE, or Integrated Development Environment, Arduino language compiler, and get everything setup as well as configured. You will find a horde of IDEs on the internet. Microsoft provides the Visual Studio as its IDE, and Apple has X code. You are welcome to use those tools, particularly if you like them. However for this book, we have chosen the Code Blocks IDE.

The great feature of Code Blocks is that it comes with everything you require. Unlike other IDEs, you don't have to hunt for this or after the IDE is set up. You just need to download, configure, and you are ready to go. Obtain Code Blocks by going to the developer.

Making the Most of Your Arduino Projects

One of the best things about the Arduino platform is that it is open-source; this is a big part of why it is so popular.

Documenting our work is essential so that we can contribute to the growing pool of knowledge. By documentation, I mean more than writing things down.

I want to talk about various tools and resources that you can use for documenting your projects and passing what you have learned on to others, as well as doing it in a manner that doesn't disrupt your work.

The code that you write for the Arduino needs to be well documented.

I feel that the most important thing is to write self-documenting code. By that, I mean that the code has intelligently named variables and functions so that someone reading the system can infer what is going on by reading the code itself.

Of course, comments are necessary and very helpful too, and good commenting practice is essential. If you are doing large projects, then you might want to consider an automated documentation system like Doxygen that has been around for a very long time.

Next, documenting the hardware, the easiest way to do this is to have pictures and videos of your project, but beyond that, some tools are handy for recording the device, such as Fritzing.

If you want to make a circuit diagram, you can also use software like Fritzing. If you are making your circuit boards, this is the way to go; I found it difficult, but a straightforward solution that I rather enjoy doing is to take some graph paper and draw the circuit myself with a pen, then scan it into my computer as an image, that might sound very clunky and old-fashioned, but I find it very efficient. It seems that no matter how hard you try, there is always some little symbol that you can't get right with software, but this is very easy when using pen and paper. I find it to be the most enjoyable part of documenting a project.

If you're writing a lot of programs, you might also want to consider using revision control software, there are many exceptional revision control systems available for free. If you are a single developer, then you may find that the old RCS (revision control system) has everything you need, and often, the simplest solution is the best solution, and it doesn't get much simpler than RCS. I think a better idea is to use something like Git, which although it's intended for large distributed projects, also works for individuals if you're willing to get past the initial learning curve. Git has a significant advantage in that it works seamlessly with Github. Github is a hugely popular source code hosting service that offers unlimited free public repositories and also gives private pools for free. This is how your tools for enabling productive work merge with tools for sharing with others.

If someone wants a copy of your code, you just give them the URL of your Git repository. You can also go with SourceForge, which is the original open-source project hosting site that existed long before Git was popular. Once you've finished a project, have a well-documented source code, and a freely available place to put your source code, you should include your other documentation e.g., circuit diagrams.

CHAPTER THREE

The Arduino Programming Language

Arduino supports a language known as the Arduino programming language, or simply Arduino language.

It is based on the Wiring development platform, which also is based on Processing, and if you are not acquainted with it, is what p5.js is based on. It's a long history of jobs building on other tasks in an extremely Open Source format. The Arduino IDE is mostly based on the Processing IDE and the Wiring IDE, which develops on it.

When we carry out any work with Arduino, we normally use the Arduino IDE (Integrated Development Environment), a software available for all the significant desktop platforms (MacOS, Linux, Windows), which gives us two things: a programming editor with integrated libraries support, a way to quickly assemble and load our Arduino programs to a board linked to the computer.

The Arduino programming language is generally a structure developed on top of C++. You can argue that it's not a genuine programming language in the traditional term, but this helps to avoid confusion for novices.

Any program written in the Arduino programming language is called sketch. A sketch is normally conserved with the .ino extension (from Arduino).

The main distinction from "typical" C or C++ is that you wrap all your code into two main functions. You can have more than two, naturally, but any Arduino program must supply not less than those two.

One is referred to as setup, while the other is called loop.

The first is called as soon as when the program begins; the second is repeatedly called while your program is running.

We don't have a primary function like you are used to in C/C++ as the entry point for a program. The IDE will make the end result is the right C++ application and will essentially add the missing out on glue by pre-processing it as soon as you compile your sketch.

Every other thing is C++ code, and as C++ is a superset of C, any legitimate C is also a valid Arduino code.

One distinction that may cause you troubles is that while you can generate your program over multiple files, those files must all remain in the same folder. Might be an offer breaking limitation if your program will grow very big, but at that, point it will be easy to transfer to a native C++ setup, which is possible.

A section of the Arduino programming language is the built-in libraries that enable you to quickly incorporate the functionality offered by the Arduino board.

Your first Arduino program will definitely include making a led turn on the light and after that switch off. To achieve this, you will use the pinMode, hold-up() and digitalWrite() functions, in addition to some regular functionalities, like HIGH, LOW, OUTPUT.

Always remember that you are not restricted to using this language and IDE to program an Arduino. Projects exist, to name a few, allow you run Node.js code on it using the Johnny Five task, Python code using pyserial and Go code with Gobot, but the Arduino programming language is definitely the one you'll see most tutorials on, given that it's the native and canonical way to deal with such devices.

The Arduino Programming Language Built-in Constants

Arduino provides two constants we can use to increase corresponds to a high level of voltage, which can vary depending on the hardware (> 2V on 3.3 V boards like Arduino Nano, > 3V on 5V boards like Arduino Uno).

LOW equates to a low voltage point. Again, the fundamental worth depends on the particular board used.

Then we have about three constants we can use in a mix with the pinMode functionality:

- INPUT presents the pin as an input pin.

- OUTPUT displays the pin as an output pin.

- The INPUT_PULLUP sets the pin as an internal pull-up resistor.

The other consistent we have is LED_BUILTIN, which indicates the variety of the on-board pin, which usually relates to the number 13.

We have the C/C++ coefficients true and false.

Arduino Math Constants

- M_PI the continuous(3.14159265358979323846).

- M_LN10 is the traditional logarithm used for the number 10.

- M_LN2 is the traditional logarithm of the number 2.

- M_LOG10E the logarithm From E to Level 10.

- M_LOG2E the logarithm of the base 2.

- M_SQRT2 the square root of 2.

- NAN the NAN (not a number) consistent.

The Arduino Programming Language Built-in Functions

In this section, I am going to refer to the integrated functions supplied by the Arduino programming language.

Program Lifecycle

- **Setup:** This function is called when the program starts, as well as when the Arduino is shut down and restarted.

- **Loop:** This function is called regularly while the Arduino system is working.

Dealing with I/O

The following functions assist with handling input and output from your Arduino gadget.

Digital I/O

- **DigitalRead()** checks out the value from a digital pin. Accepts a PIN as a parameter and returns the LOW or HIGH consistent.

- **DigitalWrite()** writes a HIGH or LOW worth to a digital output pin. You permit the PIN and LOW or HIGH as parameters.

- **PinMode** sets a pin to be an output or an input. You pass the PIN and the OUTPUT or INPUT value as parameters.

- **PulseIn()** reads a digital Pulse from WEAK to MODERATE, and then to SOFT, or from HIGH to LOW and to HIGH again on a pin. The program will block up until the pulse is identified. You specify the PIN and the sort of pulse you wish to determine (LHL or HLH). You can define an optional timeout to stop waiting on that pulse.

- **PulseInLong** is like pulseIn, other than it is implemented differently, and it can't be used if interrupts are shut off. Interrupts are typically shut off to get a more accurate outcome.

- **ShiftIn()** checks out a byte of data one bit at a time from a pin.

- **ShiftOut()** composes a byte of information one bit at a time to a pin.

- **Tone()** sends out a square wave on a pin, used for buzzers/speakers to play sounds. You can specify the frequency, pin, and it works on both analog pins and digital.

- **noTone()** stops the tone() the wave produced on a button.

Analog I/O

- **AnalogRead()** reads the value. The wave is produced on a button.

- **AnalogReference()** configures the value used for the leading input range in the analog input, by default 5V in 5V boards and 3.3 V in 3.3 V boards.

- **AnalogWrite()** writes an analog rate to a pin.

- **AnalogReadResolution()** allows you to replace the default analog bits resolution for analogRead(); by default 10 bits work on specific gadgets (Arduino Fee, No, and MKR).

- **AnalogWriteResolution()** allows you to change the default analog bits resolution to analog Write(), by default 10 bits. It only deals with specific gadgets (Arduino Charge, Zero, and MKR).

Time Functions

- **Delay()** pauses the program for a variety of milliseconds specified as a parameter.

- **DelayMicroseconds()** pauses the program for some split seconds, known as a criterion.

- **Micros()** the number of microseconds from the start of the program. Resets after ~ 70 times due to overflow.

- **Millis()**a variety of milliseconds before the start of the program, resets after ~ 50 days due to overflow.

Mathematics Functions

- **Abs()**the outright value of a number.

- **Constrain()**constrains within some range.

- **Map()**re-maps a number from one set to another; see the use.

- **Max()** the best two numbers.

- **Minutes()** the minimum of two numbers.

- **Pow()** the value and amount arose to energized.

- **Sq()** the square of the amount.

- **Sqrt()** the square root of a number.

- **Cos()** the cosine of an angle.

- **Sin()** the sine of an angle.

- **Tan()** the tangent of an angle.

Dealing with Alphanumeric Characters

- **isAlpha()** checks if a character is alpha (a letter)
- **isAlphaNumeric()** checks if a character is alphanumeric (a letter or number)
- **isAscii()** checks if a character is an ASCII character
- **isControl()** checks if a character is a control character
- **isDigit()** checks if a *'char'* is a number

- **isGraph()** checks if a *'char'* is a printable ASCII character, and contains content (it is not a space, for example)

- **isHexadecimalDigit()** checks if a *'char'* is an hexadecimal digit (A-F 0-9)

- **isLowerCase()** checks if a *'char'* is a letter in lower case

- **isPrintable()** checks if a *'char'* is a printable ASCII character

- **isPunct()** checks if a *'char'* is a punctuation (a comma, a semicolon, an exclamation mark etc)

- **isSpace()** checks if a *'char'* is a space, form feed \f, newline \n, carriage return \r, horizontal tab \t, or vertical tab \v.

- **isUpperCase()** checks if a *'char'* is a letter in upper case

- **isWhitespace()** checks if a *'char'* is a space character or an horizontal tab \t

Random Numbers Generation

- **Random()** generate a pseudo-random number.

- **randomSeed()** initialize the pseudo-random number creator with an arbitrary first figure. In Arduino, like in many languages, it's impossible to get random numbers, and the series is continuously the same, so you seed it with the present time or (in the case of Arduino) you can check out the input from an analog port.

Working with Bytes and Bits

- Bit() computes the worth of a bit (0 = 1, 1 = 2, 2 = 4, 3 = 8 ...).

- BitClear() clears (sets to 0) a small numeric variable, takes a number, and the variety of the bit beginning with the right.

- BitRead() read a little number. It accepts a number and the amount of the bit from the edge.

- BitSet() sets to 1 a little number. It accepts a number and the amount of the bit from the beginning.

- BitWrite() write one or zero to a particular bit of a number Accepts a number, the variety of the bit beginning with the right, and the value to write (zero or one).

- HighByte() get the high-order bit of the term attribute (which has 2 bytes).

- LowByte() get the low-order (rightest) byte of a vector term (comprehension)two bytes).

Disrupts

- NoInterrupts() disables interrupts.

- Disrupts() re-enables disrupts after they've been handicapped.

- AttachInterrupt() allow a digital input pin to be an interrupt. Many boards have different permitted pins; check the primary docs.

- DetachInterrupt() disables an interrupt enabled using attachInterrupt().

CHAPTER FOUR

Arduino Coding Environment and Basic Tools

What Language Is Arduino?

Arduino code is written in C++ with the addition of unique approaches and functions, which we'll mention later. C++ is a human-readable programming language. When you produce a 'sketch' (the name provided to Arduino code files), it is processed and put together to machine language.

Arduino IDE

The Arduino Integrated Development Environment (IDE) is the primary software for editing text used for Arduino programming.

It is where you'll be typing your code before uploading it to the board you want to program. Arduino code is described as sketches.

Arduino Code Example

As you can see, the IDE possesses a minimalist design. There are only five headings on the menu bar, together with a series of buttons that allow you to verify and submit your sketches. Essentially, the IDE translates and assembles your sketches to code that Arduino can understand. As soon as your Arduino code is assembled, it's then uploaded to the board's memory.

All the user needs to do this to start compiling their sketch is press the button. If there are any mistakes in the Arduino code, a warning message will flag up, prompting the user to make changes. The majority of new users typically experience difficulty with compiling because of Arduino's stringent syntax requirements. The code won't assemble, and you'll be satisfied with an error message if you make any mistakes in your punctuation when using Arduino.

Serial Monitor and Serial Plotter

The Arduino serial monitor can be started by clicking on the magnifying glass icon on the upper left side of the IDE or under tools. The serial screen is used purposely for engaging the Arduino board using the computer and is a considerable tool for real-time monitoring and debugging. To use the monitor, you will have to use the serial class.

The code you download from circuito.io possesses a position of authentication that helps you to evaluate each part using the serial display.

Arduino Serial Plotter

This is another element of the Arduino IDE, which allows you to generate a real-time chart of your serial information. The serial plotter makes it a lot easier for you to examine your information through a visual display. You're able to create graphs, negative worth charts, and conduct waveform analysis.

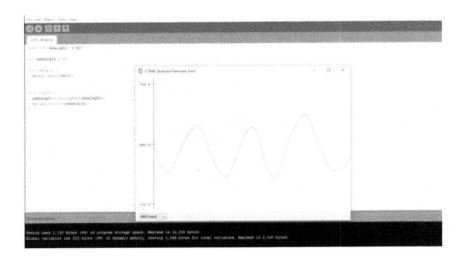

Debugging Arduino Code and Hardware

Unlike other software programming platforms, Arduino does not have an on-board debugger. Users can either use a third-party software application or serial display to print Arduino's active processes for monitoring and debugging.

By using the serial level to print, a serial programming debugs its remarks and values of variables. On many Arduino models, this will be using serial pins 0 and 1, which are connected to the USB port.

Code Structure

Libraries

In Arduino, similar to other leading programming platforms, there are built-in libraries that give basic functionality. Also, it's possible to bring in other libraries and broaden the Arduino board's abilities and functions. These libraries are approximately divided into libraries that engage with an element or those that carry out new services.

To import a brand-new library, you need to go to Sketch > Import Library on your PC.

Also, at the peak of your.ino file, you need to use '#include', which consists of external libraries. You can also create custom-made libraries to use isolated sketches.

Pin Definitions

To use the Arduino pins, you would need to identify which pin is being used and its performance. A practical way to specify the used pins is by using:

'#define pinNamepinNumber'.

The performance is either input or output and is defined by using the pinMode() technique in the setup section.

Variables

You need to declare worldwide variables and instances to be used whenever you're using Arduino.

In a nutshell, a variable enables you to name and keep a value to be used in the future. You would store data obtained from a sensor to use it later.

To declare a variable, you merely define its type, name, and initial value.

It's worth pointing out that stating global variables isn't an outright requirement, it's advisable that you declare your variables to make it easy to use your values more down the line.

Instances

In software programming, a class is a compilation of functions and variables that are kept together in one place. Each class has a particular function known as a contractor, which is used to develop an example of the class. To use the purposes of the course, we need to declare a situation for it.

Setup()

Every Arduino sketch needs to have a setup function. Once this function defines the preliminary state of the Arduino on boot and runs.

Here we'll specify the following:

- Initialize classes.

- Initialize variables.

- Preliminary state of pins.

- Pin functionality using the pinMode function.

- Code logic.

Loop()

Once setup() is done, the loop function is a must for every Arduino sketch and dos. It is the primary function, and as its name tips, it runs in a loop over and over again. The loop explains the fundamental reasoning of your circuit.

How to Configure Arduino

The basic Arduino code reasoning is an "if-then" structure and can be divided into four blocks:

1 **Setup** –Will generally be written in the setup section of the Arduino code and carries out things that need to be done as soon as possible, such as sensing unit calibration.

2 **Input** –At the start of the loop, checked out the information. These values will be applied as conditions ("if") such as the ambient light reading from an LDR using analogRead().

3 **Manipulate Data** –This is used to change the information into a more convenient form or carry out estimations. For example, the analog read() gives a reading of 0-1023, which can be mapped to a range of 0-255 to be used for PWM.

4 **Output** – This area specifies the final result of the logic ("then") according to the information determined in the previous step. Looking at an example of the LDR and

PWM, switch on an LED when the ambient light level goes down with a specific limit.

Arduino Code Libraries

Library Structure

A library is a folder consisted of files with C++ (.CPP) code files and C++ (.h) header files.

- The .h file explains the structure of the library and states all its functions and variables.

- The .cpp file holds the function application.

Importing Libraries

The first thing you need to do is identify the library you intend to use out of the many libraries available online. After downloading it to your computer, you need to open Arduino IDE and click Sketch > Include Library > Manage Libraries.

You can then select the library that you would like to import into the IDE. Once the process is complete, the library will be provided in the sketch menu.

In the code supplied by circuito.io, instead of including external libraries, as discussed previously, we provide them with the firmware folder. In this case, the IDE knows the method of finding them when using #include.

From Software to Hardware

There is a lot to be stated about Arduino's software application capabilities, but it's crucial to remember that the platform consists of both software and hardware. The two operate in tandem to run a complicated operating system.

Code > Compile > Upload > Run.

At the core of Arduino is the capability to run the code and compile.

After writing the code in the IDE, you need to release it to the Arduino. Clicking the Upload button (the right-facing arrow icon) will compile the code and upload it if it passed collection. As soon as your upload is complete, the program will start running automatically.

You can also do this action by step:

1 First of all, assemble the code. To do this, click the check icon (or click on sketch)> Verify/Compile in the menu bar.

2 When you've done this, Arduino will begin to compile. Once it's finished, you'll get a completion message.

3 If your code fails to run, you'll also be informed, and the problematic code will be highlighted for editing.

4 As soon as you've compiled your sketch, it's time to upload it.

5 Pick the serial port your Arduino is currently connected to. To do this, click on "Tools">"Serial Port" in the menu to select it; you can then publish the assembled sketch.

6 To submit the sketch, click on the upload icon next to the tick. Additionally, you can go to the menu and click File >Upload. When the data is being moved, your Arduino LEDs will flicker.

7   When complete, you'll be greeted with a conclusion message that tells you Arduino has ended up uploading.

Establishing Your IDE

To link an Arduino board to your computer, you need a USB cable. When using the Arduino UNO, the USB transmits the data in the program straight to your board. The USB cable is used to power the Arduino. You can also run your Arduino effectively through an external source of energy.

Before you can upload the code, there are specific settings that you would need to configure.

Choose your board –You have to designate which Arduino board you're going to be using. Do this by clicking Tools > Board > Your Board.

Select your processor, there are specific boards (for example Arduino pro-mini) of which you need to define which processor you will use. Under tools >Processor >Choose the plan you have.

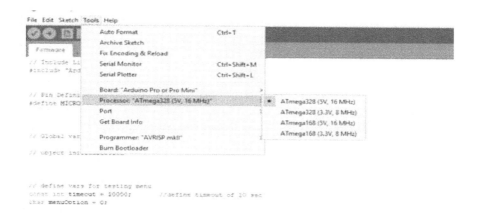

Pick your port – To select the port to which your board is linked, go to Tools > Port > COMX Arduino (this is Arduino's serial port).

How to Install Non-Native Boards

Some board types and designs are not pre-installed in the Arduino IDE; therefore, you'll need to install them before you can upload code.

To install a non-native board such as NodeMCU, you would need to:

1   Click on tools > Boards > Boards Manager.

2   Look for the board you wish to add the search bar and click "install".

Some boards cannot be found through the Board Manager. In this case, you'll need to include them manually. To do this:

1   Click on Files > Preferences.

2   In the Additional Boards Supervisor field, paste the URL of the installation bundle of your board. For instance, for NodeMCU,   add   the   following: URL:http://arduino.esp8266.com/stable/package_esp8266 com_index.json.

3   Click OK.

4   Go to tools > Boards > Boards Manager.

Search for the board you wish to add in the search bar and click "install".

When you've completed this step, you will see the setup boards in the boards' list under tools.

Note: The process may vary a little for different boards.

Arduino: An Extremely Versatile Platform

Arduino is far more than a simple microcontroller. With an expansive IDE and a wide variety of hardware setups, Arduino is genuinely a diverse platform. The type of its libraries and its instinctive style make it a preferred for new users and knowledgeable makers alike. There are countless community resources to assist you in getting started with both hardware and software applications.

As you advance your abilities, you may face problems that require debugging, which is a weak area of the Arduino IDE. Thankfully, there are several methods and tools to debug any Arduino hardware and software application.

CHAPTER FIVE

Why We Choose Arduino, What Can We Do with It?

Arduino is a rapid electronic prototyping platform made up of the Arduino board and the Arduino IDE.

What Is Arduino?

It is an open-source task; software/hardware is very available and very flexible to be tailored and extended.

It is versatile, uses a range of digital and analog inputs, SPI, serial user interface, digital and PWM outputs.

It is simple to use, connects to the computer through USB and communicates using the basic serial procedure, runs in standalone mode and as interface linked to PC/Macintosh computer systems.

It is economical, around 30 euros per board and comes with a free authoring software application.

Arduino is backed up by a developing online community, many source code is already offered, and we can share and post examples for others to use, too!

I ought to note that many of the developers of Arduino are based in Ivrea, merely 40 minutes from Torino, where we lie: calling, networking, and collaborating with them in the future can be pretty straightforward.

What Can I Make with an Arduino?

Practically anything you want! It has been made use of in so many ways as the alternatives are virtually unlimited.

i   Past tasks included robotics, art setups, in-car computer systems, MIDI controllers, cocktail makers, human-computer user interfaces, Facebook 'Like' counters, marketing screens, clocks, song instruments, customized computer mouse and keyboard, home automation... The list continues!

ii The highlights of an Arduino board are its capacity to review information from sensing units, to send out and get digital signals as well as attach using serial to your computer system.

iii You can manage many things, from LEDs and LCDs to electric motors and relays.

iv You can also read values from sensors such as potentiometers, light-dependent resistors (LDRs), and piezos.

v   The digital pins on an Arduino allow you to check out or compose 5Vvalues.

vi You can use a pin to switch on an LED (with a resistor).

vii You can send a signal to a relay to run higher voltage home appliances like televisions and house lights. You can send messages to electric motors to switch on and off.

viii You can inspect to see if a button has been pressed.

ix You can even send and get serial data, identical information, and electronic pulse width inflection, virtually anything that can be regulated via a little current.

The analog pins permit you to review an incoming voltage between 0V and 5V. This will be exactly how you check out from sensing units. There are a plethora of sensing units readily available, from accessible, hands-on pressure sensing units and rotary potentiometers, to environment sensors such as pressure, gas, temperature level, and alcohol. If you have, for example, a slider set to exactly half of its variety, it ought to result in a voltage of 2.5V. The Arduino can read this and use the value to control another object.

You do not have to stop with merely regulating electronic circuits. You can send data back to the computer to manage software such as Handling and Max/MSP. You can send out the data on USB with most designs. Some models have Bluetooth and Ethernet ports, together with an extra shield (like an add-on device) you can communicate through Wi-Fi and other methods.

What Can We Finish with Arduino?

Arduino is a terrific tool for establishing interactive items, taking inputs from a variety of switches or sensing units, and managing a range of lights, motors, and other outputs. Arduino projects can stand-alone, or they can be connected to a computer system using USB.

The Arduino will be regarded as a simple serial user interface (do you remember the COM1 on Windows?). There are serial communication APIs on many programming languages, so interfacing Arduino with a software application running on the computer system should be quite straightforward.

The Arduino board: A microcontroller module, a little circuit board(the board) that contains a whole computer system on a bit of chip (the microcontroller). There are various versions of the Arduino board; they are different in components, objective and size, etc. Some examples of Arduino boards include Arduino Diecimila, Arduino Duemilanove, Freeduino, Arduino NG, and many more. Arduino schematics are distributed using a free certificate to make someone complimentary to build his

Arduino compatible board. The Arduino name is a registered trademark; this will disallow you from calling your hacked board Arduino.

Arduino Duemilanove

I was given an Arduino Duemilanove board, which is, according to the Arduino developers, the most basic one to use and the best one for learning.

A vital element of the Arduino board is the number of connectors readily available. These are the components which allow circuitry the Arduino boards to other parts (sensors, resistors, buttons, and more) that can be connected: reading, composing, moving, etc.

Arduino Duemilanove board has the following connectors (noted clockwise beginning from the leading left):

AREF: Analog Reference Pin
The voltage at this pin figures out the voltage at which the analog-to-digital converters (ADC) will report the decimal worth 1023, which is their highest level output. This suggests

that using this pin, you'll have the ability to change the maximum value readable by the analog in nails; this is a way to change the scale of the analog in pins.

The AREF pin is, by default, connected to the 5V AVCC voltage (unless you are running your Arduino at a lower voltage).

GND: Digital Ground

Used as ground for digital inputs/outputs.

DIGITAL 0-13: Digital Pins

Used for digital I/O.

Digital pins have different uses.

TX/RX Pins 0-1: Serial In/Out

These pins can be used for digital I/O just like it's done with digital pins 2-13, but they can't be used for serial communication.

If your work uses serial communication, you might wish to use the one for Serial interaction instead of using the USB to the serial user interface. This can be useful while using the serial user interface to interact with a no PC gadget (e.g., another Arduino or a robot controller).

External Interrupts Pins 2-3

These pins can be configured to set up an interrupt on different input conditions. I still did not know how to use these pins, but more information is readily available on the attachInterrupt() function referral.

PWM Pins 3, 5, 6, 9, 10, 11.

Provide 8-bit PWM output alongside the analogWrite() function.

LED: 13

There is an integrated LED linked to digital pin 13. When the pin is HIGH value, the LED is switched on; when the pin is LOW, it's off.

ICSP: In-circuit Serial Programmer

Arduino comes with a bootloader, which makes it possible for program uploading through the USB to the serial interface. Advanced users can also directly submit programs to the

Arduino board using an external programmer. This is done using the ICSP header, by doing so you save the ~ 2KB memory used in submitting sketches logic.

ANALOG IN 0-5: Analog Input Pins

They are used to read from an analog source (for example, a pressure sensing unit or potentiometer).

POWER Pins

Used to get or supply power to the Arduino board.

Vin

When using an external power supply, this offers the same current, which is showing up from the power supply. It's likewise possible to give voltage through this pin.

Grand (2 Pins)

Used as ground pins for your tasks.

While searching for the distinctions between the digital ground and the other two ground pins, I discovered that all the three ground pins on the Arduino board are connected; therefore the digital ground pin and the two ground pins under the power section are the same. I didn't examine the Arduino Duemilanove interior style on this.

- **5V:** This is used to acquire 5V power from the board. This is the same thing that powers the microcontroller. This can be as a result of USB or Vin (external power supply).

- **3V3:** A 3.3V power supply which is created from the FTDI chip. The optimum existing draw is 50mA. If subjected to small or large current draws, as read in the forum, it shows that the FTDI chip is quite a delicate part that can quickly burn. The consensus is to prevent using this pin source of power.

- **RESET:** By bringing this line to LOW, you can reset the board; there is also a button for doing so on the board but, as additional guards (e.g., Ethernet shield) may make the button unreachable, this can be used for resetting the board.

- **External Power Supply In:** With this, we can link an external power supply to Arduino. A 2.1 mm centre-positive plug connected to a battery or an AC-to-DC adapter. The current range can be 6 to 20 volts, however in order not to get too hot and stability problems, the advised variety is seven to twelve volts.

- **USB:** Used for publishing sketches (Arduino binary programs) to the board and serial interaction between the board and the computer system. Arduino can be powered from the USB port.

What Can't I Perform with One?

The Arduino doesn't have a great deal of processing power, so virtually any kind of significant intensive task is out of the inquiry. You will not have the ability to process, document, or output video or audio (although you can output graphics to TFT or LCD screens). It is not like a computer system. You will not be able to connect your webcam or keyboard to it. There is no operating system with a GUI (like a Raspberry Pi). It is a different quiet monster.

Can Anyone Make Use of One?

That's the charm of it. Even if you have no understanding or experience with electronic devices or shows, you can get a primary job and run in one or two hours.

Getting a result in a flash on and off in a pattern is as simple as adding an LED and resistor to a breadboard, connecting some cables, and composing some code lines. Arduinos are used in classrooms throughout the globe as a starter in programming and electronics.

The Arduino KIT

Arduino Board is pretty useless until we connect it to different electrical components. Usually, coupled with an Arduino board, stores also give Arduino KITs, which consists of many useful elements for developing circuits with Arduino.

I was supplied with an Arduino Base Workshop KIT, which contains:

- 1 x Straight single line pinhead connectors 2,54 40x1.

- 1 x Arduino Duemilanove board.

- 5 x 10K Ohm Resistors 1/4W (brown, orange, black, gold).

- 1 x USB cable.

- 5 x 2.2K Ohm Resistor 1/4 W (red, red, red, gold).

- 10 x 220 Ohm Resistors 1/4W (red, red, gold brown).

- 5 x 100nF capacitor polyester.

- 5 x 10nF capacitor polyester.

- 3 x 100uF electrolytic capacitor 25Vdc.

- 1 x 4,7K Ohm Thermistor.

- 5 x 330K Ohm Resistors 1/4W (orange, orange, yellow, gold).

- 1 x 10..40K Ohm LDR VT90N2.

- 3 x 5mm RED LED.

- 1 x 5mm GREEN LED.

- 1 x 5mm YELLOW LED.

- 1 x 10K Ohm linear potentiometer, PCB terminals.

- 2 x BC547 Transistor in TO92 Package.

- 1 x Set of 70 breadboard jumper wires.

- 1 x Piezo buzzer.

- 5 x PCB Pushbutton, 12x12mm size.

- 2 x 4N35 Optocoupler DIL-6 bundle.

- 1 x Breadboard, 840 tie points.

- 2 x Tilt sensor.

- 1 x Diode 1n4007.

- 1 x MOS Irf540.

Arduino IDE

The other part of the Arduino forum is Arduino IDE. This includes all the software which will run a computer to program and interact with an Arduino board.

The Arduino IDE contains an editor that is used for sketching (that's the name of Arduino programs); in short, the Arduino programming language imitated the processing language.

Using the IDE, the program we composed is converted to C language and then compiled using Avr-GCC. This procedure produces binary code which the microcontroller on the Arduino board will be able to perform and understand.

When the Arduino board is linked to a computer using the USB cable, by using the IDE, we can compile and upload to the jury the program.

Arduino and Linux

Archlinux system had no problems in the Arduino board when connected to a PC.A new Linux device called /dev/ttyUSB0 is produced.

If you have other devices linked using USB, which uses serial communication (e.g., a 3G UMTS USB dongle), you should carefully check the gadget name that your Arduino gets (you can use does for this). Other USB devices will also get a /dev/tty

USBX gadget, so the Arduino may end up using a different gadget name (e.g., /dev/ttyUSB5) if/ dev/USB0 is not given (use mesg after plugging Arduino to check how Arduino was named).

In this case, perhaps you want a checklist for the Arduino board always ends up called with the same name.

CHAPTER SIX

A Tour of the Arduino UNO Board

You can try various electronic parts but don't have adequate knowledge, then Arduino is what you need to proceed.

So what is Arduino?

Arduino is a microcontroller-electronic prototyping platform based on open software that can be set with a user-friendly Arduino IDE.

This chapter will discuss what's on the Arduino UNO board and what it can do. UNO is not the only board in the Arduino collection. There are some other boards like Arduino Mega, Arduino Lilypad, Arduino Mini, and Arduino Nano.

However, the Arduino UNO board ended up being more popular than other boards in the household because it has more comprehensive documentation. This led to high adoption for electronic prototyping, producing a large neighborhood of electronic geeks and hobbyists.

In recent times, the UNO board is known as Arduino.

Components of Arduino UNO Board

The significant parts of the Arduino UNO board are as follows:

- USB adapter

- Power port

- Microcontroller

- Reset switch

- Crystal oscillator

- Analog input pins

- Digital pins

- USB interface chip

- TX RX LEDs

Now let's take a better look at each part:

USB adapter: This is a printer USB port used in loading a program from the Arduino IDE to the Arduino board. The board can likewise be powered through this port.

Power port: An AC-to-DC adapter or a battery can power the Arduino board. The power supply can be connected by plugging in a 2.1 mm centre-positive plug into the power jack of the board. The Arduino UNO board runs at a voltage of 5 volts, but it can endure a maximum voltage of 20 volts. If the board is provided with a higher voltage, there is a voltage regulator (it sits between the power port and USB port) that safeguards the board from stressing out.

Microcontroller: An Atmega328P microcontroller. It is the most prominent black rectangular chip, which comprises twenty-eight pins. Consider it as the brain behind your Arduino. The microcontroller used on the UNO board is Atmega328P by Atmel (major microcontroller producer).

Atmega328P has the following components in it:

- Flash memory of 32KB. The program loaded from Arduino IDE is kept here.

- RAM of 2KB. This is a runtime memory.

CPU: It manages everything that goes on within the gadget. It fetches the program instructions from flash memory and executes them with the help of a RAM.

Electrically Erasable Programmable Read-Only Memory (EEPROM) of 1 KB: This is a form of non-volatile memory, and it keeps the data after the device restarts and resets.

Atmega328P is pre-programmed with a bootloader. This allows you to directly submit a new Arduino program into the gadget without using any external hardware developer, making the Arduino UNO board easy to use.

Analog input pins: The Arduino UNO board has six analog input pins, known as "Analog 0 to 5."

These pins can read the signal from an analog sensing panel as a temperature level sensing unit and convert it to a digital value so that the system understands. These pins determine voltage and not the present because they have a very high internal resistance. Hence, just a percentage of present circulations through these pins.

These pins are identified as analog inputs by default. These pins can also be used for digital input or output.

Digital pins: You can discover these pins identified "Digital 0 to 13." These pins can be used as either output or input pins. When used as an output, these pins function as a power supply source for the components connected to them. When used as input pins, they check out the signals from the part attached to them.

When digital pins are used as output points, they contain forty milliamps of current at five volts, which is sufficient to light an LED.

Some of the digital pins are identified with the tilde (~) symbol next to the PINs (PINs 3, 5, 6, 9, 10, 11).

These pins act as optical sticks but can be used for Pulse-Width Modulation (PWM), which mimics analog output like fading an LED in and out.

Reset switch: When this switch is clicked, it gives a sound vibration to the reset pin of the Microcontroller and runs the program from the start. This can be extremely helpful if your code doesn't repeat, but you wish to evaluate it several times.

Crystal oscillator: This is a quartz crystal oscillator which ticks sixty million times in a second. On each tick, the microcontroller does one operation, for instance, addition, subtraction, and so on.

USB user interface chip: Consider this as a signal translator. It transforms signals in the USB level to a level that an Arduino UNO board understands.

TX-RX LEDs: TX means transmit, and RX for receive. These are indicator LEDs that blink anytime the UNO board is sending or getting data.

Now that you have explored the Arduino UNO board, you have started your journey towards developing your first IoT prototype.

CHAPTER SEVEN

Arduino – Overview

Arduino is a prototype platform (open-source) based on user-friendly hardware and software. It includes a circuit board, which can be programmed (referred to as a microcontroller) and a ready-made software called Arduino IDE (Integrated Development Environment), which is used to write and publish the computer system code to the physical board.

Key Function of Arduino

The essential functions are:

- Arduino boards can read analog or digital input signals from various sensing units and turn it into an output such as triggering a motor, turning LED on/off, connect to the cloud, and many other actions.

- You can control your board functions by sending some instructions directly to the microcontroller located on the board via Arduino IDE (described as uploading software application).

- Unlike many previous programmable circuit boards, Arduino does not need an extra piece of hardware (called a programmer) to pack a brand-new code into the board. You can simply use a USB cable.

- Additionally, the Arduino IDE makes use of a simplified version of C++, making it easier to discover the program.

- Finally, Arduino provides a standard type element that breaks the functions of the micro-controller into a more available plan.

Board Types

Various kinds of Arduino boards are readily available, depending on the different microcontrollers used. However, all Arduino boards have one thing in common; they are known to be programmed through the Arduino IDE.

The differences are the variety of outputs and inputs (the number of buttons, LEDs, and sensing units you can use on a single board), speed, running voltage, kind aspect, etc. Some boards are designed to be ingrained and have no programming interface (hardware), which you would need to buy personally. Some can run directly from a 3.7V battery, and others require a minimum of 5V.

Here is a list of several Arduino boards available:

- Arduino boards based on ATMEGA328 microcontroller
- Arduino boards based on ATMEGA32u4 microcontroller
- Arduino boards based on ATMEGA2560 microcontroller
- Arduino boards based on AT91SAM3X8E microcontroller

CHAPTER EIGHT

Arduino – Board Description

In this chapter, we will discover the different parts contained on the Arduino board. Since it is the most widely known board in the Arduino board family, we will study the Arduino UNO board.

In addition, it is the best board to begin coding and electronics. Some boards look a bit different from the one given below; however, many Arduinos have a lot of these parts in common.

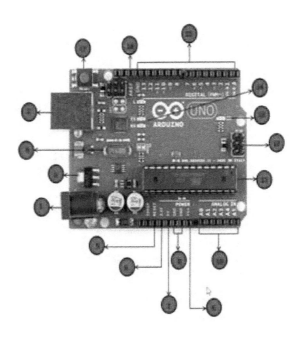

Power USB

Arduino board can be driven by using the USB cable from your computer system. All you need to do is connect the USB cable properly to the USB connection.

Power (Barrel Jack)

Arduino boards can be powered right from the air conditioner's main power supply by connecting it to the barrel jack (2).

Voltage Regulator

The function of the voltage regulator is to control the voltage given to the Arduino board and stabilize the DC voltages used by the processor and other elements.

Crystal Oscillator

The crystal oscillator assists Arduino in dealing with time concerns.

How Does Arduino Compute Time?

The answer is by using the crystal oscillator. The number printed on the Arduino time is 16,000H9H. It tells us that the frequency is 16 MHz or 16,000,000 Hertz.

The Arduino Reset

You can reset your Arduino board, that is, begin your program from the beginning. You can reset the UNO board in two ways.

- By using the reset control (17) on the screen.

- By connecting an external reset button to the Arduino pin labeled RESET (5).

Pins (3.3, 5, GND, Vin)

- 3.3 V (6)—Supply 3.3 output volt.

- 5V (7)—Supply 5 output volt.

- Most of the parts used with the Arduino board work better with 3.3 volts and 5 volts.

- GND (8)(Ground)—There are many GND pins on the Arduino, any of which can be used to ground your circuit.

- Vin (9)—This pin also can be used to power your Arduino board right from an external power source, like air conditioner's main power supply.

Analog Pins

The Arduino UNO board has six analog input pins A0 through A5. The volts can check out the signal from an analog sensing unit like the humidity sensor or temperature level sensor and transform it into a digital value that can be checked by the microprocessor.

Main Microcontroller

Each Arduino board has its microcontroller (11). You can take it as the brain of your board. The main IC (integrated circuit) on the Arduino is a little different from one board to another. The microcontrollers are generally from the ATMEL Company. You must know what IC your board has before filling up a new program from the Arduino IDE. This detail is available on the top of the IC. For more information about the IC building and functions, you can refer to the information sheet.

ICSP Pin

Mainly, ICSP (12) is an AVR, a small programming header for the Arduino consisting of MOSI, MISO, SCK, RESET, VCC, and GND. It is typically described as an SPI (serial peripheral interface), which could be considered as the "growth" of the output. You are working the output device to the master of the SPI bus.

Power LED Indication

When you plug your Arduino into a power source to confirm that your board is well powered up, this LED ought to light up.

There is something wrong with the connection if this light does not switch on.

AREF

AREF stands for analog reference. It is often used to set an external referral voltage (between 0 and 5 volts) as the upper limit for the analog input pins.

Arduino – Installation

After discovering the main parts of the Arduino UNO board, we are all set to learn how to set up the Arduino IDE. Once we learn this, we will be ready to upload a program properly on the Arduino board.

Ways to Set up the Arduino IDE on Your Computer

In this section, you have the opportunity to learn how to set up the Arduino IDE on our computer system and prepare the board to receive the program through USB cable.

Step 1 – Firstly, you should have your Arduino board (you can choose your favourite board) and a USB cable. In case you use Nano, Arduino Mega 2560, Arduino UNO, Arduino

Duemilanove, or Diecimila, you will need a standard USB cable (A plug to B plug).

Step 2 – Download Arduino IDE Software. You can get different varieties of Arduino IDE from the download page on the Arduino official website. You must choose your software application, which works with your OS (Windows, IOS, or Linux). After your file download is done, unzip the file.

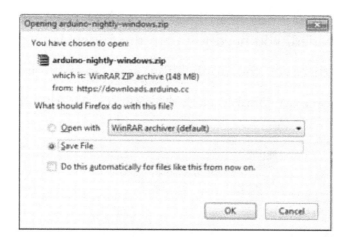

Step3– Power up your board. The Arduino Uno, Arduino Nano Mega, Duemilanove, and immediately draw power from either the USB connection to the computer or an external power supply. If you are using an Arduino Diecimila, you have to

make that the board is set up to draw power from the USB connection. The source of energy is chosen with a jumper, a small piece of plastic that fits two of the three pins between the USB and power jacks. Examine that it is on the two pins closest to the USB port.

Link the Arduino board to your computer using the USB cable. The green power LED (labeled PWR) should be radiant.

Step 4 – Launch Arduino IDE. After your Arduino IDE software is downloaded, you need to unzip the folder. Inside the folder, you can discover the application icon with an infinity label (application.exe). Double-click the image to start the IDE.

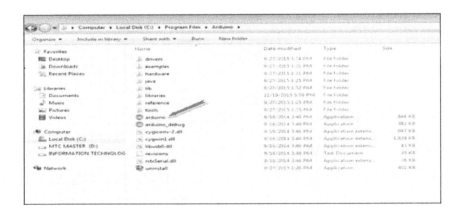

Step 5 – Open your first task. When the software starts, you have two alternatives:

- Create a new task.

- Open an existing task example.

To create a brand-new job, select File > New.

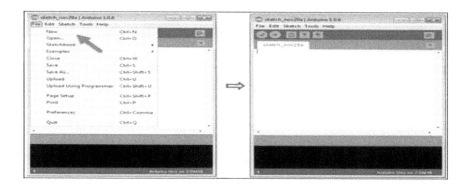

To open an existing project example, choose File > Example > Basics > Blink.

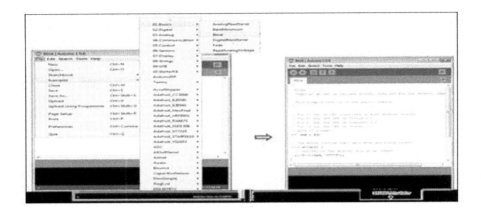

Here, we are choosing among the examples with the name Blink. It turns the LED off and on with some hold-up. You can pick any other instance from the list.

Step6– Select your Arduino board.

To avoid any error while submitting your program to the board, you should choose the appropriate Arduino board name, which matches with the board connected to your computer system.

Go to Tools > Board and choose your board.

Here, we have selected the Arduino Uno board; however, you should choose the name matching the board that you are using.

112

Step 7 – Select your serial port. Select the serial gadget of the Arduino board. Go to Tools > Serial Port menu. This is likely to be COM3 or greater (COM1 and COM2 are usually reserved for hardware serial ports). To find out, you can disengage your Arduino board and re-open the menu, the entry that disappears need to be of the Arduino board. Reconnect the board and select that serial port.

113

Step 8 – Upload the program to your board. Before highlighting how we can publish our application to the board, we should demonstrate the function of each symbol appearing in the Arduino IDE toolbar.

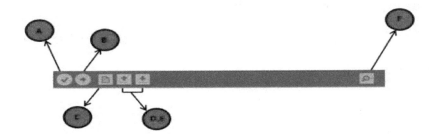

A – Used to check any compilation error.

B – Used to upload programs to the Arduino board.

C – Shortcut used to produce a new sketch.

D – Used to straight open among the example sketch.

E – Used to save your sketch.

F – Serial screen used to receive serial information from the board and send the following information to the board.

Now, merely click the "Upload" button in the environment. Wait a few seconds; you will see the TX LEDs and RXbon on the

114

board flashing. If the upload achieves success, the message "Done publishing" will appear in the status bar.

Note: If you have an Arduino Micro or other board, NG, you need to press the reset button physically on the board right away before clicking the upload button on the Arduino software.

Arduino – Program Structure

In this session, we will study the Arduino program structure, and we will discover more new terminologies used in the Arduino world. The Arduino software application is open-source. The source code for the Java environment is launched below the GPL, and the C/C++ microcontroller libraries are under the LGPL.

Sketch

The first brand-new term in the Arduino program is "sketch".

Arduino programs can be split into three main parts:

1. Structure

2. Values (variables and constants)

3. Functions

In this session, we will learn more about the Arduino software application program, step by step, and how we can write the program without any syntax or collection mistake.

Let us begin with the structure. The software application structure consists of two primary functions:

- Setup() function

- Loop() function

PURPOSE

The **setup()** function is called when a sketch starts. Use it to initialize the variables, pin modes, start using libraries, etc. The setup function will only run once, after each power up or reset of the Arduino board.

After creating a **setup()** function, which initializes and sets the initial values, **the loop()** function does precisely what its name suggests, and loops consecutively, allowing your program to change and respond. Use it to actively control the Arduino board.

Arduino – Data Types

Information types in Arduino refer to a comprehensive system used for stating variables or functions of various kinds. The type of variable identifies how much space it occupies in the storage and how the bit pattern saved is analyzed.

Below are the data types that you need during Arduino programming:

Void

The space keyword is used only in function declarations. It shows that the function is anticipated to return no details to the role from which it was called.

Example

Space Loop

Boolean

A Boolean holds one of two values, right or wrong. Each Boolean variable inhabits one byte of memory.

Example

boolean value = incorrect;// declaration of variable with type boolean and initialize it with falseboolean state = real;// declaration of variable with type boolean and initialize it with true

Char

An information type that takes one byte of memory that saves a character worth, character literals are written in single quotes.

However, characters are saved as numbers. You can see the particular encoding in the ASCII chart. This indicates that it is possible to do math operations on aspects in which the ASCII worth of the role is used. For example, 'A' + 1 has worth 66 because the ASCII value of the uppercase A is 65.

Example

Char chr_a='a';// statement of a variable with type char and initialize it with a character a.

Char chr_c = 97;// declaration of a variable with type char and initialize it with character 97.

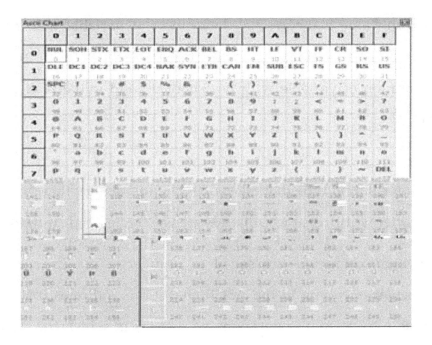

Unsigned Char

Anonymous char is an unsigned data type that occupies one byte of memory. The unknown char data type encodes numbers from 0 to 255.

Example

Anonymous Char chr_y = 121;// statement of the variable with type Unsigned char and initialize it with character y.

Byte

A byte stores an 8-bit unknown number, from 0 to 255.

Example

Byte m = 25;// declaration of a variable with type byte and initialize it with 25.

Int

Integers are the main data-type for number storage. Int stores a 16-bit (2-byte) worth. This yields a series of -32,768 to 32,767 (minimum value of $-2 \wedge 15$ and a maximum amount of $(2 \wedge 15) - 1$).

The intsize varies from one board to another. On the Arduino Due, for instance, an int shops a 32-bit (4-byte) worth. This yields a series of -2,147,483,648 to 2,147,483,647 (minimum worth of -2 ^ 31 and an optimum value of (2 ^ 31) - 1).

Example

int counter = 32;// declaration of a variable with type int and initialize it with 32.

Unsigned Int

Anonymous ints (unsigned integers) are the same as an int in the manner in which they store a 2-byte value. Instead of keeping negative numbers, nevertheless, they only stay positive values, yielding a beneficial series of 0 to 65,535 (2 ^ 16) - 1). The Due stores a 4 byte (32-bit) value, within the zero to four,294,967,295 (2 ^ 32 - 1).

Example

Anonymous int counter = 60;// declaration of a variable with type unsigned int and initialize it with 60.

Word

On the Uno and other ATMEGA based boards, a word becomes a 16-bit unsigned number. On the Due and Zero, it keeps a 32-bit unsigned number.

Example

Word w = 1000;// declaration of a variable with type word and initialize it with 1000.

Long

Long variables are extended size variables adopted for number storage, and store 32 bits (4 bytes), from -2,147,483,648 to 2,147,483,647.

Example

High speed = 102346;// statement of a variable with type Long and initialize it with 102346.

Anonymous Long

Unsigned long variables are extended size variables for number storage and shop 32 bits (4 bytes). Compare to longs, and anonymous longs will not save negative numbers, making their range from 0 to 4,294,967,295 (2 ^ 32 - 1).

Example

Anonymous Long speed = 101006;// declaration of a variable with type Unsigned Long and initialized it with 101006.

Short

A petite one is a 16-bit data-based on every Arduino. (ATMega and ARM-based), a small stores a 16-bit (2-byte) value. This results a variety of -32,768 to 32,767 (minimum value of -2 ^ 15 and an optimum worth of (2 ^ 15) - 1).

Example

Brief Val = 13;// statement of a variable with type short and initialize it with 13.

Float

Information type for the floating-point number is a number that has a decimal point. Floating-point names are frequently used to approximate the analog and constant values because they have higher resolution than integers.

Floating-point numbers can be as small as -3.4028235 E +38 and as large as 3.4028235 E +38. They are stored as 32 bits (4 bytes) of details.

Binary

Other ATMEGA based and Uno boards.

Double-precision floating-point number occupies four bytes. That is, the dual implementation is the same as the float, without benefits in precision. On the Arduino Due, doubles have 8-byte (64 bit) accuracy.

Example

Statement of variable double num = 45.352;// with type double and start it with 45.352.

CHAPTER NINE

Arduino–Variables and Constants

Before we begin discussing the variable types, there is a crucial subject we need to make sure you understand quite well; this is called the variable scope.

What Is a Variable Scope?

The variables in Arduino programming language, those that Arduino uses, have a residential or commercial property called scope. A scope is a region of the program, and there are three locations where the declaration of variables can be made. They are:

- Inside a block or a function, which is called regional variables.

- In the definition of function parameters, which is called formal places.

- Outside every feature, which is called global variables.

Regional Variables

The variables that are stated inside a function or block are regional variables. They can be used by the statements that are inside that function or block of code. Local variables are not known to function outside their own.

Following is the example using local variables:

- Void setup ()

- Space loop ()

```
Void setup (){

}

Void loop (){
intx, y ;
intz;Local variable declaration
  x =0;
  y =0; actual initialization
```

```
  z =10;
}
```

Global Variables

Global variables are defined beyond all the functions, generally at the top of the program. The global variables will hold their worth throughout the lifetime of your plan.

Any function can access a global variable; that is, you can use the above during your entire program after its declaration.

The following example uses regional and global variables:

```
IntT, S ;
float c =0;Global variable declaration


Void setup (){


}


Void loop (){
intx, y ;
```

```
intz;Local variable declaration

x =0;

y =0; actual initialization

z =10;}
```

Int T, S;

float c = 0; Global variable declaration

Space setup ()

Void loop ()

Arduino – Operators

An operator is a sign that informs the compiler to carry out specific mathematical or sensible functions. C language is rich in integrated operators and provides the following kinds of operators:

- Arithmetic Operators

- Comparison Operators

- Boolean Operators

- Bitwise Operators

- Substance Operators

Arduino –Control Structures

Decision making structures need that the developer specifies one or more conditions to be evaluated or checked by the program. It must be along with a declaration or statements to be executed if the state is determined to be real, and additionally, other announcements to be carried out if the state is determined to be false.

Following is the essential kind of a typical choice-making structure found in most of the programming languages:

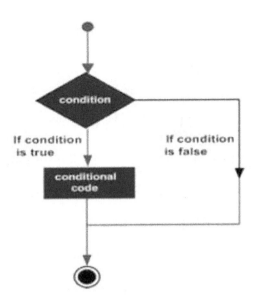

Control structures are elements in the source code that control already made program.

They comprise of:

Arduino – Loops

Languages in programming give different control structures that provide more complicated execution paths.

A loop declaration allows us to carry out a statement or group of accounts many times, and the following is the basic form of a loop declaration in the majority of the programming languages:

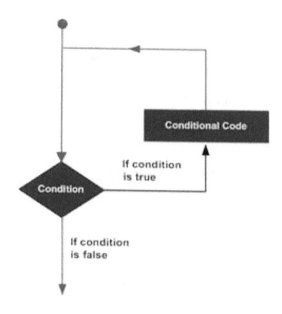

Arduino – Functions

Functions allow structuring the programs in sectors of code to carry out private jobs. The typical case for creating a service is when one needs to carry out the same action many times in a program.

- Functions codify one step in one place so that the roles need to be considered once.

- Standardizing code fragments into services has many benefits.

- Features help the programmer stay arranged. Often this helps to conceive the program.

- This also reduces possibilities for mistakes in adjustment if the code needs to be altered.

- Functions make the whole sketch smaller and more compact.

There are two functions in an Arduino sketch, i.e., setup () and loop(). Other features should be created outside the brackets of these two functions.

The most common syntax to specify a function is:

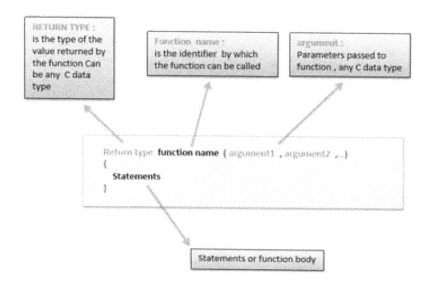

Function Declaration

A function is declared outside any other features.

Which are:

Firstly, writing the part of the function known as a function prototype above the loop function, which consists of:

- Function return type.

- Function name.

- Function argument type, no requirement to write the argument name.

Function model should be followed by a semicolon (;).

The copying reveals the presence of the function declaration using the first method.

The second part, which is called the function definition or statement, needs to be declared below the loop function, which consists of:

- Function return type.

- Function name.

- Function argument type, here you need to include the argument name.

- The function body (declarations inside the function are carrying out when the function is called).

Low Power Arduino

A usual Arduino, for example, the Mini does not consume much power, commonly 40 MA when connected to a USB cable. If you're going to be powering your Arduino on something aside from batteries, the power requirements usually aren't a concern; it will undoubtedly be inadequate to make any type of distinction. Once you start something like a remote monitoring application where you are needed to run with battery power, power consumption can become substantial.

In my functioning experience, hoping to calculate the number of time an Arduino will continue with a battery pack is reasonably tight because there are many variables included, types of alkaline, nickel-metal hydride, lithium-ion, rechargeable, non-rechargeable for a specific kind of battery state triple-A, there will be widely varying storage abilities depending on the design of battery it is (nickel-metal hydride or lithium-ion). There is irregularity amongst the different brands (usually you obtain what you spend for). When your batteries depleted, the voltage provided decreases; if you are using four three-way A batteries, which supply six volts to operate an Arduino which calls for at least 5V, the Arduino might effectively stop working when the voltage provided dips and low, even when there is a substantial amount of power remaining in the batteries.

I will not be doing any kind of details computations below for the reason that I discover the figures are not sensible. I have to state that batteries typically are defined in regards to milliampere hours. So anytime your Arduino is connected through USB, it's working at 5 volts; if it is attracting forty milliamperes, that isn't the same action of wattage as requiring forty milliamperes from a 9V battery. Moreover, it depends on what your application is. Are you just taking input from some kind of analog surveillance tool, or are you using it on a servo? These have drastically different power requirements, and again in my experience, you'll discover it not helpful to determine. I place the most effective method is to find some batteries you have around the house and also see how long they last after used those dimensions to make empiric calculations.

Presume you're dealing with a remote monitoring device, and you need to have the Arduino to gauge something for some significant time continuously. I did something comparable with a DS18B20 sensor that was within one of the cold frames in my lawn; it would have been a discomfort drawing an expansion cable bent on the park, and not an excellent suggestion to leave it outdoors revealed, so I pick operating on a battery.

The ATmega, as well as SAM processors that come on an, Arduino contain some extremely advanced power administration functionality that you can play with. Still, before we review the techniques which you can make your Arduino preserve power, we need to analyze some simple direct services. Most importantly, it would be to use a different Arduino that is feasible. The 3.3 volt Arduinos will use less energy than a 5V Arduino for a specific kind of application. The Arduino Nano and Arduino Micro will use less power than a Uno and Mega, and if they benefit your demands, this alone may be enough.

Another point to think of is using a different kind of battery. Currently, when we mention batteries, it occasionally seems as if there is this attitude that lithium-ion batteries are the best for anything. Lithium-ion batteries are lovely for possessing a very high power/weight ratio.

This is wonderful for tasks like robots and various other things that move. If your battery isn't going to move, a better option might be a lead-acid battery, similar to the one in your vehicle or truck; this is what I decided on in my yard cold frame.

What if you still want to conserve power and a different Arduino or larger sized battery will not meet your requirements? Then there are lots of approaches we can try out to get the Arduino to conserve power.

One technique is to bypass everything except the processor chip; you do this by avoiding the power connector but directly give energy to the processor with power. You must be careful here that you stay inside the operating limitations of the given chip which is on your Arduino, that voltage regulator is for a reason! This will save significant power. The processor chip consumes much less energy than the entire Arduino board; this is typically in the form of heat lost by the regulator and objects like the LED.

- Another way to reduce power consumption is to lower the clock speed. If you're running a program like monitoring the temperature of your frame every thirty seconds, there's no need for the Arduino to perform at its maximum clock rate. This can be accomplished with the pre-scaler library. You can reduce the clock speed by a factor as much as 256; this will decrease a sixteen megahertz Arduino to a 62.5 kHz one, but when you find yourself just checking a measurement every 25 seconds or so, this is more than enough, and this will decrease consumption significantly.

- For a remote monitoring project, the most effective technique you could do to improve efficiency is to put Arduino to sleep. There is a library called narcoleptic, which allows you to hold the Arduino in a minimal consumption mode, and just a single timer is functioning. This timer can be used to awaken the Arduino every 20 seconds, as I needed to do. Many of the smaller 3.3V Arduino's will consume under 1 MA while asleep.

Adding Ethernet, Wi-Fi, and Other Communications to Your Arduino (or Other PIC) – Including the NSLU2

The Arduino is a small programmable device that can hold a short program and perform tasks such as reading temperature sensors, turning on or off switches, and can serve as the 'brain' for a robot. I have used the Arduino (actually freeArduino) for projects related to HVAC and hydroponics automation.

It is often useful to communicate with the Arduino—for example, everyday use of an Arduino is for data collection. You may have a temperature sensor wired to the Arduino and interface with flash storage to log the temperature data. Later you have to remove the flash storage and transfer it to your computer.

What If You Can Communicate with the Arduino?

With Ethernet or wireless connectivity, you could simply connect to the Arduino with a computer and capture the data in real-time. This gives more automation and opens a world of possibilities; real-time alerts, real-time adjustments (have the Arduino switch something on/off), and many more.

There Are Some Choices Available for Communications

Serial: The Arduino has TTL lines, not traditional RS232, but it is possible for a reasonable cost to use a conversion/level adapter or circuit. You could then run a serial line to a computer. This is acceptable in many cases but restricts you to using one network, and in the case of my home, the wiring is not as convenient. I have Ethernet cat5 running all over the place, so if I am going to use a wired solution, Ethernet is the best.

Wi-Fi: For some, this may be the best solution. If you cannot or do not want to run wires of any kind, solutions are ranging from 400/900 MHz transceivers that use 4-6 pins for simple communications to more powerful XBee, ZigBee, and even 802.11 Wi-Fi. The primary issue I have found with these solutions is the cost or the technical expertise required. Also, double-check if the interface you are using requires any libraries or interface code that will use space within the Arduino. The RFM units are promising as they are low cost, though I have not successfully interfaced them as of yet.

Ethernet: There are some solutions for adding Ethernet capabilities such as shields and serial to Ethernet bridges/adapters. Some require a 'TCP/IP stack' to be written to the Arduino—consider this as it uses many storage spaces.

NSLU2 or Computer: For my application, I chose to use some NSLU2 units I had (these are often available via online auction). The NSLU2 is a network-attached storage device (NAS) that is frequently changed (hacked) to run other operating systems and improve its functionality at the hardware level. In my case, I overclocked mine and installed Debian Linux using an 8GB flash drive. The NSLU2 also uses a TTL interface, though at 3.3V instead of 5V. Interfacing is done with three simple wires, and a resistor is needed on one line for the 3.3V to 5V conversion.

This book has presented several options for adding communications capabilities to the Arduino.

CHAPTER TEN

Arduino – Strings

This is used to store text. They can be used to show text on an LCD or in the Arduino IDE serial monitor window. Strings are also helpful for keeping user input.

- Two kinds of strings in Arduino programming.

- The Arduino String, which gives room for sketching.

- Arrays of characters, which are the same as strings.

String Arrays Character

The first type of string that we will find out is the string that is a series of characters of the type char. In the previous chapter, we learned what an array is, a consecutive sequence of the same kind of variable saved in memory. A string is a variety of char variables.

A string is a unique range that has one additional component at the end of the series, which always has a value of 0 (absolutely no). This is referred to as a "null ended string".

String Character Array Example

This will demonstrate how to make a string and print it to the serial display window.

void loop()

The following example reveals what a string is made up of; a character selection with characters 0 as the last component of the range to show that this is where the string ends. The string can be printed out to the Arduino IDE serial monitor window by using Serialprintln() and passing the name of the string.

Example

charmy_str[]="Hello";.

Serial.begin(9600);.

void setup()

Serial.println(my_str);.

space loop()

In this sketch, the compiler determines the string size, string selection, and the string null terminations. A selection that is six aspects long and includes five characters followed by an absolutely no is produced with the same method as in the previous sketch.

Manipulating String Arrays

We can modify a string array within a sketch, as revealed in the following illustration.

Example

```
voidsetup(){
charlike[]="I like coffee and cake";// create a string
Serial.begin(9600);
// (1) print the string
Serial.println(like);
// (2) delete part of the string
like[13]=0;
Serial.println(like);
```

```
// (3) substitute a word into the string
like[13]=' ';// replace the null terminator with a space
like[18]='t';// insert the new word
like[19]='e';
like[20]='a';
like[21]=0;// terminate the string
Serial.println(like);
}


voidloop(){


}
```

Result

I like coffee and cake.

I like coffee.

I like coffee and tea.

The sketch operates in the following way:

Producing and Printing the String

In the sketch given above, a new string is produced and printed for the screen in the serial monitor window.

Shortening the String

The string is shortened by replacing the 14th character in the chain together with a valueless terminating zero (two). This is component number 13 in the string variety counting from 0.

When the string is printed, all the characters are written to the new null ending.

Other characters do not disappear; they still exist in memory, and the string selection remains the same size. The only difference is that any function that works with strings will only see the chain up to the first null terminator.

Changing a Word in the String

Finally, the sketch changes the word "cake" with "tea" (3). It first has to replace the null terminator at like [thirteen] with a place where the string is brought back to the initially developed format.

New characters overwrite "cak" from the word "cake" with the "tea".

This is done by excessive writing of specific characters in ex. The 'e' of "cake" is replaced with a brand-new null ending character. The outcome is that it ended with two invalid characters, the original one at the end of the string and the new one that changes the 'e' in "cake". This makes no difference when the unique chain is printed because the function that writes the string stops printing the string characters when it comes across the very first null terminator.

Functions to Manipulate String Arrays

The previous sketch manually manipulated the string by accessing special characters in the chain. To make it much easier to control string arrays, you can compose your functions to do so or use some of the string operations from the C language library.

Provided Below Is the List of Functions to Manipulate String Arrays

The next sketch uses some Arduino string functions.

Example

```
voidsetup(){

charstr[]="This is my string";// create a string

charout_str[40];// output from string functions placed here

intnum;// general purpose integer

Serial.begin(9600);


// (1) print the string

Serial.println(str);


// (2) get the length of the string (excludes null terminator)

num=strlen(str);

Serial.print("String length is: ");

Serial.println(num);


// (3) get the length of the array (includes null terminator)
```

```
num=sizeof(str);// sizeof() is not a C string function
Serial.print("Size of the array: ");
Serial.println(num);


// (4) copy a string
strcpy(out_str,str);
Serial.println(out_str);


// (5) add a string to the end of a string (append)
strcat(out_str," sketch.");
Serial.println(out_str);
num=strlen(out_str);
Serial.print("String length is: ");
Serial.println(num);
num=sizeof(out_str);
Serial.print("Size of the array out_str[]: ");
Serial.println(num);
}


voidloop(){}
```

Result

This is my string.

String length is 17.

Size of the selection: 18.

This is my string.

This is my string sketch.

String length is25.

Size of the range out_str []: 40.

The sketch operates in the following method:

Print the String

The newly developed string is printed to the serial monitor window, as carried out in previous sketches.

Get the Length of the String

The string line() function is used to get the string length, which is used for the printable characters only and not the null terminator.

The string contains 17 characters.

Get the Length of the Range

The operator sizeof() is used to get the string length. The length includes the null terminator, so the distance is more than the length of the string.

Sizeof() appears like a function; however, technically is an operator. It is not part of the C string library but was used in the sketch to indicate the distinction between the size of the range and the size of the string (or string length).

The string was copied to the range for us to have an extra space in the selection to use in the next part of the sketch that is including a string to the end.

Add a String to a String (Concatenate)

The sketch joins one string to another. This is done by using the string() function. The chain() feature puts the second string passed to it to the end of the first team.

Concatenation, the length of the string is printed to show the brand-new string length. The length of the range is then written to show that we have a 25-character long line in a 40 aspect long range.

Bear in mind that the 25-character long string uses up 26 characters of the array due to the null ending zero.

Selection Bounds

When dealing with strings and varieties, it is essential to work within the bounds of chains or selections. In the example sketch, a variation was created, which was 40 characters long to allocate the memory that could be used to manipulate strings.

If the selection was made smaller and we tried to copy a string that is larger than the range to it, the chain would be replicated at the end of the selection. The memory beyond the end of the collection could include other relevant information used in the sketch, which would then be overwritten by our string. If the mind beyond completion of the chain is overrun, it could crash the design or cause unanticipated behavior.

Arduino – String Object

The second type of string is object string, which can be used in Arduino programming as well.

What Is an Object?

An object is a construct that contains both data and functions. A String object can be produced merely like a variable and assigned a value or string. The String object includes features (which are called "approaches" in objects oriented programming 'OOP') that run on the string information contained in the String object.

The following sketch and explanation will make it clear what an item is and how the String object is used.

Example

```
voidsetup(){
Stringmy_str="This is my string.";
Serial.begin(9600);

// (1) print the string
```

```
Serial.println(my_str);

// (2) change the string to upper-case
my_str.toUpperCase();
Serial.println(my_str);

// (3) overwrite the string
my_str="My new string.";
Serial.println(my_str);

// (4) replace a word in the string
my_str.replace("string","Arduino sketch");
Serial.println(my_str);

// (5) get the length of the string
Serial.print("String length is: ");
Serial.println(my_str.length());
}

voidloop(){}
```

Result

This is my string.

THIS IS MY STRING.

My brand-new string.

My new Arduino sketch.

String length is 22.

A string object is developed and appointed a worth (or string) at the top of the sketch.

String my_str="This is my string.";.

This develops a String object with the name my_str and gives it a value of "This is my string".

This can be compared to creating a variable and assigning a worth to it such as an integer:

intmy_var = 102;.

The sketch works in the following way.

Printing the String

The string can be printed to the serial monitor window just like a character array string.

Change the String to Uppercase

The String objectmy_str that was created has a variety of functions or ways that can be run on it. These methods are invoked by using the object's name followed by the dot operator (.) and the name of the function to use.

my_str. toUpperCase();.

The toUpperCase() function runs on the string consisted of my_str object, which is of type String and transforms the string information (or text) that the objects contain to upper-case characters. A list of the functions that the String class consists of can be found in the Arduino String reference. Technically, String is called a level and is used to create String objects.

Overwrite a Series

The job operator is used to appoint a brand-new string to the my_strobjects that replace the old string.

my_str="My brand-new string.";.

The project operator cannot be used on character variety strings, however, it deals only with String objects.

Changing a Word in the String

The replace() function is used to replace the first string passed to it by the second string pass. return() is another function that is constructed to the String class and is readily available to use on the String objectsmy_str.

Getting the Length of the String

This is very easy to do with the uses of length().

In the sample sketch, the result returned by length() is passed directly to Serial.println() without using an intermediate variable.

When You Can Use a String Object

A String object is easier to use than a string character array. The objects have integrated functions that can perform a variety of operations on strings.

The primary downside of using the String object is that it uses a great deal of memory and can rapidly use up the Arduinos RAM, which might cause Arduino to hang and crash all of a sudden. If a sketch on an Arduino is little and limits making use of objects, then there ought to be no problems.

Character array strings are more challenging to use, and you may need to compose your functions to run these types of lines. The advantage is that you have control over the size of the string ranges that you make, so you can keep the fields small to save memory.

You need to make sure that you do not compose beyond the end of the range bounds with string varieties. The String object does not have this problem and will look after the string bounds for you, providing enough memory for it to run on. The String object can attempt to write memory that does not exist when it lacks memory but will not write on the end of the string that it is operating on.

CHAPTER ELEVEN

Stating Arrays

Ranges inhabit an area in memory. To define the type of aspects and the number of components required by a range, use a declaration of the following:

Type arrayName [arraySize];

The compiler reserves the proper quantity of memory. (Recall that a declaration, which reserves memory is more meaning).

The array size must be an integer consistent greater than nothing. To tell the compiler to reserve 11 aspects for integer variety C, use the statement:

int C [12];// C is a variety of 12 integers

Selections can be declared to contain the values of a non-reference data type. A range of type string can be used to keep character strings.

Examples Using Arrays

This section offers many examples that show how to state, start, and control varieties.

Example 1: Declaring an array and using a loop for array's elements.

Lines a—b is the use or statement to initialize the selection components to nos. Like other automated variables, automatic arrays are not implicitly initialized to absolutely no. The first output declaration (line c) displays the column headings for the columns printed in the subsequent for a confirmation (lines e), which writes the selection in tabular format.

Pins Configured as INPUT

Arduino pins are configured as inputs, so they do not need to be called data with pinMode() when you are using them as inputs. Pins configured by doing this are stated to be in a high-impedance state. Input pins make minimal demands on the circuit equals to a series of 100 megaohms in front of the nail.

This suggests that it takes minimal current to change the input pin from one state to another. This makes the pins beneficial for such jobs as carrying out a capacitive touch sensing unit or reading an LED as a photodiode.

Pins set up as pinMode(pin, INPUT) with a wire that is not connected to other circuits, or without anything to connect them, report seemingly random changes in the state of the pins, getting electrical noise from the environment, or capacitive coupling the state of a neighboring pin.

Pull-up Resistors

If no input is present, pull-up resistors are typically useful to steer an input pin to a known state. This can be done by adding a pull-up resistor (to +5V)on the input.

Important Features

Here are some crucial functions about disrupts:

- Most Arduino styles have two hardware interrupts (described as "interrupt0" and "interrupt1") hard-wired to digital I/O pins 2 and 3, respectively.

- The Arduino Mega has six hardware disrupts, including the extra disrupts ("interrupt2" through "interrupt5") on pins 21, 20, 19, and 18.

- You can specify a routine using a particular function called "Interrupt Service Routine" (generally referred to as ISR).

- Interrupts can originate from various sources. In this case, we are using a hardware interrupt that is generated by a state change in the digital pins.

- You can define the regular and specify conditions at the rising edge, falling edge, or both. At these specific conditions, the interrupts would be addressed.

Types of Interrupts

We have two types of disrupts:

- Hardware Interrupts – They occur in response to an external occasion, like an external interrupt pin going low or high.

- Software Interrupts – They occur in action to a guideline sent out in software. The only kind of interrupt that the "Arduino language" supports is the attachInterrupt() function.

Using Interrupts in Arduino

Interrupts are beneficial in Arduino programs as it assists in resolving timing problems. A useful application of an interrupt reads a rotary encoder or observing a user input. Generally, an ISR must be fast and as brief as possible. If your sketch uses several ISRs, only one can perform at a time. Other interrupts will be carried out after the current one finishes in an order that depends upon the concern they have.

Usually, global variables are used to pass data between an ISR and the main program. To ensure variables shared between an ISR and the first program are updated properly, declare them as unstable.

attachInterrupt Statement Syntax

attachInterrupt(digitalPinToInterrupt(pin), ISR, mode);// suggested for Arduino board attachInterrupt(pin, ISR, mode);// suggested Arduino Due, Zero only

// argument pin: the PIN

// argument ISR: the ISR to call when the interrupt happens

// This function is often referred to as an interrupt service regimen.

// argument mode: defines when the interrupt ought to be activated.

The following three constants are predefined as legitimate values:

- FALLING anytime the pin goes from high to low.

- LOW to activate the interrupt whenever the pin is low.

- CHANGE to trigger the interrupt whenever the pin changes its value.

Communication in Arduino

Many communication methods have been specified to achieve this data exchange. Each procedure can be classified into one of the two classifications: parallel or serial.

Identical Communication

The same connection between the Arduino and peripherals using input/output ports which is the suitable option for much shorter distances to longer meters. Nevertheless, in other cases, when it is needed to develop interaction between two gadgets for longer distances, it is not possible to use a parallel connection. Identical user interfaces move multiple bits at the same time. They typically call for buses of information—sending across eight, sixteen, or more cables. Data is transferred in quantum, collapsing waves of both 1 as well as 0.

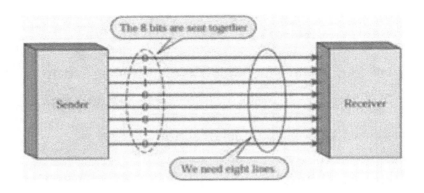

Benefits and Disadvantages of Identical Communication

Identical communication has its advantages. It is much faster than serial, uncomplicated, and relatively simple to carry out. However, it calls many input/output (I/O) ports and lines. If you needed to relocate a project from a fundamental Arduino Uno to a Mega, you recognize that the I/O lines on a microprocessor can be valuable.

Therefore, we like serial communication, compromising prospective speed for the pins.

Serial Interaction Components

Today, a lot of Arduino boards are built with some systems for serial interaction as conventional equipment.

Any of the systems used depends on the elements listed below:

- How many tools the microcontroller has to exchange data with?

- How fast the data exchange needs to be?

- What is the range between these devices?

- Is it required to send and receive information simultaneously?

Among the essential things worrying serial interaction is the protocol, which needs to be strictly observed. It is a set of regulations, which need to be used such that the devices can appropriately translate the information they mutually exchange. Luckily, Arduino makes sure that the work of the programmer/ user is decreased to simple create (information to be sent out) and read (received data).

Types of Serial Communications

Serial communication can be additional categorized as:

- **Synchronous** – Tools that are synchronized using the same clock, and their timing is in synchronization with each other.

- **Asynchronous** –Tools that are asynchronous have their own clocks and are caused by the result of the previous state.

It is easy to know if a tool is synchronous or not. If the same clock is given to all the connected devices, then they are synchronous. If there is no clock line, it is asynchronous.

The asynchronous serial method has some built-in policies.

These policies are nothing but systems that ensure robust and error-free data transfers. These systems, which we get for eschewing the exterior clock signal, are:

- Synchronization bits

- Information bits

- Parity bits

- Baud rate

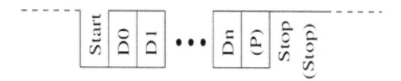

Synchronization Bits

The little synchronization bits are two or three individual bits transferred with each packet of information. They are the start and the stop bits. According to their name, these little bits note the beginning and the end of a package specifically.

There is continuously one start bit; however, the variety of stop bits is configurable to either one or two (though it is usually left at one).

To start small is always shown by an idle information line going from one to zero, while the stop bits will shift back to the idle state by holding the line at one.

Information Bits

The amount of data in each packet can be set to any size from five to nine little bits. The standard information size is your primary 8-bit byte; however other dimensions have their uses. A 7-bit information package can be much more reliable than 8, especially if you are simply transferring 7-bit ASCII personalities.

Parity Bits

The user can choose whether there should be a parity bit or not, and if so, whether the equality should be rare or not. The parity bit is 0 if the variety of 1 is among the information bits as well. Odd parity is just the contrary.

Baud Rate

The term baud rate is used to denote the variety of bits moved every second [bps];note that it refers to little bits, not bytes. It is generally called for by the protocol that each byte is transferred together with several control bits. It indicates that byte in serial data stream might include 11 little bits. For instance, if the baud rate is 300 bps, then the maximum 37 and also minimal 27 bytes may be moved per second.

Arduino – Inter-Integrated Circuit

Inter-integrated circuit (I2C) is a system for serial data exchange between the specialized integrated circuits and microcontrollers of a brand-new generation. It is used when the distance between them is short, and the connection is established via two conductors. One is used for data transfer and the other is used for synchronization (clock signal).

As seen in the adhering number, one device is constantly a master. It performs addressing of one slave chip before the communication begins. This way, one microcontroller can communicate with 112 various gadgets. The baud rate is 100 KB/s (typical setting) or 10 KB/s (slow-moving baud rate mode). Solutions with the baud rate of 3.4 MB/s have lately shown up. The range between tools, which communicate over an I2C bus is restricted to numerous meters.

Board I2C Pins

The I2C bus comprises of two signals—SCL and also SDA. SCL is the clock signal, and also SDA is the data signal. The current bus master always produces the clock signal. Some slave tools may require the clock low sometimes to delay the master sending extra information (or to need even more time to prepare data before the master attempts to clock it out). This is called "clock stretching".

Adhering to the pins for different Arduino boards:

- Uno, Pro Mini A4 (SDA), A5 (SCL).

- Huge, Due 20 (SDA), 21 (SCL).

- Leonardo, Yun 2 (SDA), 3 (SCL).

Arduino I2C

We have two modes; master code and slave. They are:

- Master Transmitter/Slave Receiver.

- Master Receiver/Slave Transmitter.

Master Transmitter/Slave Receiver

Let us see what master transmitter and slave receiver is.

Master Transmitter

The following functions are used to boot up the cord collection and also sign up with the I2C bus as a master or servant. This is normally called just once.

- Wire.begin(address) – Address is the 7-bit slave address in our situation as the master is not stated, and it will sign up with the bus as a master.

- Wire.beginTransmission(address) – Begin a transmission to the I2C slave gadget with the given address.

- Wire.write(worth) – Queues bytes for transmission from a master to servant device (in-between calls to beginTransmission() and end transmission()).

- Wire.endTransmission()–Ends a transmission to a slave device that was begun by beginTransmission() as well as transmits the bytes that were queued by wire.write().

Example

#include <Wire.h>// consist of cord library.

void arrangement()// this will certainly run just as soon as

Wire.begin();

brief age = 0;.

void loop()

Slave Receiver

```
#include<Wire.h>//include wire library


voidsetup()//this will run only once {
Wire.begin();// join i2c bus as master

}


short age =0;
```

```
voidloop(){
Wire.beginTransmission(2);
// transmit to device #2
Wire.write("age is = ");
Wire.write(age);// sends one byte
Wire.endTransmission();// stop transmitting
delay(1000);
}
```

The complying with features are used:

- **Wire.begin(address)** –Address is the 7-bit servant address.

- **Wire.onReceive(gotten data trainer)** – Feature to be called when a servant gadget obtains information from the master.

- **Wire.available()** – Returns the variety of bytes available for retrieval with Wire.read(). This need to be called inside the Wire.onReceive() handler.

Master Receiver/Slave Transmitter

Let's see what a master receiver and slave transmitter is.

Master Receiver

The master is set to request and then reads bytes of information that are sent from the distinctively addressed Servant Arduino.

The following function is used:

Wire.requestFrom(address, variety of bytes) –Used by the master to request bytes from a servant gadget. The bytes may be gotten afterward with the wire.available() and wire.read() functions.

Slave Transmitter

The following feature is used:

Wire.onRequest(handler) – A function is called when a master needs information from the servant device.

Arduino – Serial Peripheral User Interface

A Serial Peripheral User Interface (SPI) bus is a system for serial communication, which uses four conductors, commonly three. One conductor is used for getting information, one for sending out data, one for synchronization, and one alternatively for selecting a tool to interact with. It is a full-duplex connection, which shows that the data is sent and obtained at once. The maximum baud rate is more than that in the I2C communication system.

Board SPI Pins

SPI uses the complying with four cords:

- **SCK** – This is the serial clock driven by the master.

- **MISO** – This is the master input/slave output driven by the master.

- **SS** –This is the slave-selection cable.

The following features are used:

You have to include the SPI.h.

- **SPI.begin()** –Initializes the SPI bus by establishing SCK, MOSI, and SS to outcomes, pulling SCK and also MOSI reduced, and SS high.

- **MOSI** – This is the master-slave/output input driven by the master.

- **SPI.setClockDivider(divider)**–To establish the SPI clock divider panel relative to the system clock. On AVR based boards, the dividers available are 2, 4, 8, 16, 32, 64,and 128. The default setup is SPI_CLOCK_DIV4, which sets the SPI clock to one-quarter of the frequency of the system clock (5 MHz for the boards at 20 MHz).

- **SPI.beginTransaction(SPISettings(speedMaximum, data order, data mode))**–Speed maximum is the clock, data order(MSBFIRST or LSBFIRST), data model(SPI_MODE0, SPI_MODE1, SPI_MODE2, or SPI_MODE3).

- **Divider panel**– It could be (SPI_CLOCK_DIV2, SPI_CLOCK_DIV4, SPI_CLOCK_DIV8, SPI_CLOCK_DIV16, SPI_CLOCK_DIV32, SPI_CLOCK_DIV64, SPI_CLOCK_DIV128).

- **SPI. Transfer (Val)** – SPI transfer is based on a synchronized send as well as obtainment: the obtained information is returned in received Val.

We have four modus operandi in SPI as follows:

- **Setting 0 (the default)** – Clock is generally reduced (CPOL = 0), and the data is tasted on the transition from reduced to high (leading edge) (CPHA = 0).

- **Setting 1** –Clock is generally reduced (CPOL = 0), and the information is experienced on the shift from high to reduced (tracking side) (CPHA = 1).

- **Setting 2** – Clock is usually tall (CPOL = 1), and the data is tasted on the change from high to reduced (leading edge) (CPHA = 0).

- **Setting 3** – Clock is typically tall (CPOL = 1), as well as the information is tested on the change from low to high (routing edge) (CPHA = 1).

- **SPI.attachInterrupt(handler)** – Feature to be called when a slave gadget gets information from the master.

Now, we will undoubtedly connect two Arduino UNO boards, one as a master and the other as a servant.

- **(SS):** pin 10.

- **(MOSI):** pin 11.

- **(MISO):** pin 12.

- **(SCK):** pin 13.

The ground is common. Following is the diagrammatic representation of the connection between both the boards.

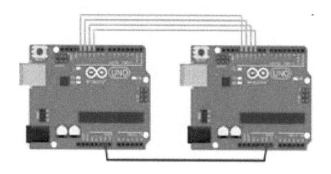

Arduino – Attaching Switch Over

Pushbuttons or switches connect two open terminals in a circuit. This instance activates the BAITED pin 2 when you press the pushbutton connected to pin 8.

Pull-down Resistors

Pull-down resistors are made use of in electronic logic circuits to make sure that inputs to Arduino work out at expected logic levels if external gadgets are separated or are at high-impedance. As nothing is attached to an input pin, it does not mean that it is an absolute no. Pull-down resistors are connected between the appropriate pin on the device and the ground.

An instance of a pull-down resistor in an electronic circuit is shown in the following figure. A pushbutton switch is connected between the supply voltage and a microcontroller pin. In such a course, when the button is shut, the micro-controller input is at a high rational worth. Yet, when the switch is open, the pull-down resistor pulls the input voltage to the ground (logical zero value), preventing an undefined state at the input.

The pull-down resistor should have a more significant resistance than the resistance of the logic circuit; otherwise, it may pull the voltage down, and the input voltage at the pin would undoubtedly continue to be at a continuous logical reduced value, despite the button position.

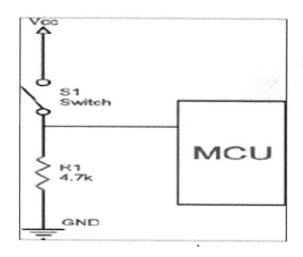

Parts Required

You will need the following components:

- One × Arduino UNO board.

- One × 330 ohm resistor.

- One × 4.7K ohm resistor (pull-down).

- One × LED.

Procedure

Adhere to the circuit layout and make the connections, as shown in the image below.

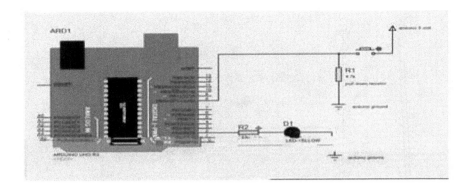

Sketch

Open the Arduino IDE software program on your computer, the coding in the Arduino language will undoubtedly manage your circuit. Open a new illustration document by clicking "New".

Arduino Code

// constants won't change. They're used here to

// set pin numbers:

constintbuttonPin=8;// the number of the pushbutton pin

constintledPin=2;// the number of the LED pin

```
// variables will change:
int buttonState=0;// variable for reading the pushbutton status


void setup(){
// initialize the LED pin as an output:
pinMode(ledPin, OUTPUT);
// initialize the pushbutton pin as an input:
pinMode(buttonPin, INPUT);
}


void loop(){
// read the state of the pushbutton value:
buttonState=digitalRead(buttonPin);
// check if the pushbutton is pressed.
// if it is, the buttonState is HIGH:
```

```
if(buttonState== HIGH){
// turn LED on:
digitalWrite(ledPin, HIGH);
}else{
```

```
// turn LED off:
digitalWrite(ledPin, LOW);
}}
```

Code to Note

When the switch is open (pushbutton is not pressed), there is no connection between the two terminals.

So the pin is connected to the ground (through the pull-down resistor), and we read a LOW. When the switch is closed (pushbutton is pressed), it makes a connection between its two terminals, attaching the pin to 5 volts, to make sure that we read a HIGH.

Result

LED is switched on when the pushbutton is pressed and switch off when it is launched.

Arduino – DC Motor

In this phase, we will use various kinds of electric motors with the Arduino board (UNO) and show how to connect the engine as well as drive it from your board.

There are three different types of motors:

- DC motor.

- Servo motor.

- Stepper electric motor.

1. A DC electric motor (direct current electric motor) is one of the most common types of engines. DC electric motors usually have two leads, one favourable and one adverse. If you connect these two leads straight to a battery, the driver will rotate.

If you change the leads, the electric motor will rotate in the contrary direction.

The pull-down resistor needs to have a more significant resistance than the impedance of the logic circuit; otherwise, it could draw the voltage down, and the input voltage pin would remain at a consistent logical low value, despite the switch setting.

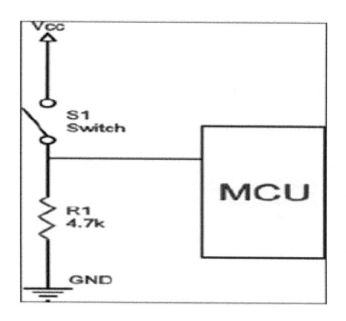

Parts Required

You will require the adhering to elements:

- One × Arduino UNO board.

- One × 330 ohm resistor.

- One × 4.7 K ohm resistor (pull-down).

- One × LED.

Procedure

Adhere to the circuit layout as well as make the links as displayed in the photo given listed below.

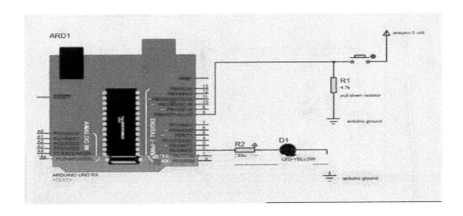

Sketch

Open up the Arduino IDE software program on your computer system. Coding in the Arduino language will regulate your circuit. Open a brand-new sketch document by clicking "New".

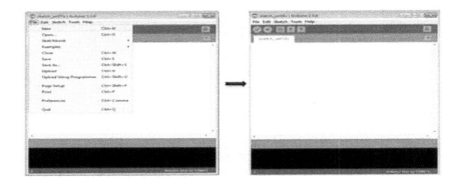

Warning: Do not drive the electric motor directly from Arduino board pins. This might damage the board. Use a chauffeur circuit or an IC.

We will split this chapter right into three parts:

- Just make your motor spin.

- Control electric motor rate.

- Control the instructions of the turn of DC electric motor.

Components Required

You will undoubtedly need to comply with these elements.

- 1x Arduino UNO board.

- 1x PN2222 Transistor.

- 1x Little 6V DC Electric Motor.

- 1x 1N4001 diode.

- 1x 270 Ω Resistor.

Treatment

Comply with the circuit representation and make the connections as displayed in the image provided below.

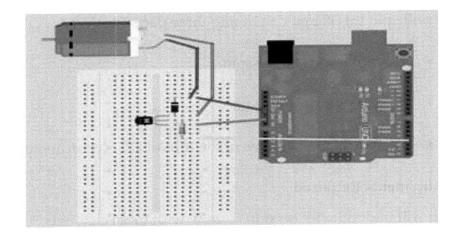

Safety Measures

Take the following preventative measures while making the connections.

- Firstly, ensure that the transistor is connected correctly. The flat side of the transistor should encounter the Arduino board as displayed in the arrangement.

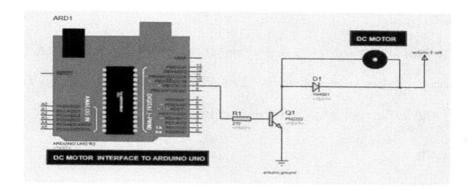

Secondly, the striped end of the diode ought to be towards the +5V power line according to the setup shown in the photo.

Spin Control Arduino Code

```
intmotorPin=3;

voidsetup(){

}

voidloop(){
digitalWrite(motorPin, HIGH);}
```

Code to Note

The transistor imitates a switch, managing the power to the motor. Arduino pin three is used to turn the transistor on and off and is named 'motorPin' in the illustration.

Result

The motor will ultimately rotate the speed when the Arduino pin three goes high.

Electric Motor Rate Control

Below is the schematic representation of a DC electric motor connected to the Arduino board.

Arduino Code

```
intmotorPin=9;


voidsetup(){
pinMode(motorPin, OUTPUT);
Serial.begin(9600);
while(!Serial);
```

```
Serial.println("Speed 0 to 255");

}
```

```
voidloop(){
if(Serial.available()){
int speed =Serial.parseInt();
if(speed >=0&& speed <=255){
analogWrite(motorPin, speed);
}
}}
```

When the program begins, it motivates you to offer the values to manage the speed of the motor. You need to go into a value between 0 and 255 in the serial monitor. In the 'loophole' feature, the command 'Serial.parseInt' is used to check out the number went into the message in the serial monitor as well as transform it right into an 'int'. You can use any kind of number here. The 'if' statement in the following line merely does an analog compose with this number if the number is between 0 and 255.

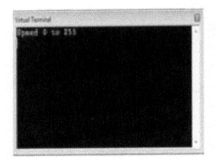 

Result

The DC electric motor will spin with various rates according to the value (0 to 250) obtained using the serial port.

Rotate Instructions Control

To manage the direction of the spin of the DC electric motor without interchanging the leads, you can use a circuit called an H-Bridge. An H-bridge is a digital circuit that can drive the automobile in both instructions. H-bridges are made used indifferent applications. One of the most usual forms is to manage motors in robots. It is called an H-bridge because it makes use of four transistors attached in such a way that the schematic diagram appears like an "H".

We will be using the L298 H-Bridge IC here. The L298 can control the instructions and the speed of DC electric motors and stepper electric motors, as well as can control two electric motors all at once. Its current score is 2A for each motor. At these currents, nevertheless, you will need to make use of warmth sinks.

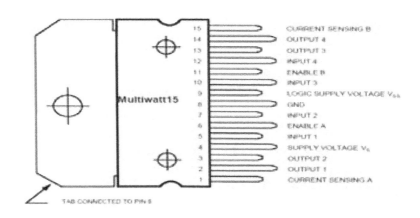

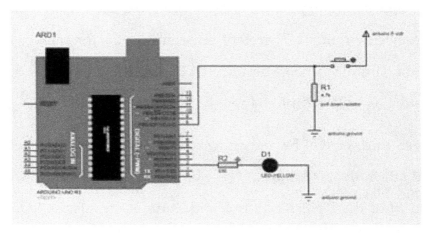

Components Required

You will certainly need the adhering parts:

- One × L298 bridge IC.

- One × DC motor.

- One × Arduino UNO.

- One × breadboard.

- 10 × jumper cables.

Procedure

Following is the schematic representation of the DC electric motor interface to the Arduino Uno board.

The above diagram shows how to attach the L298 IC to regulate two electric motors. There are three input pins for each electric motor, Input1 (IN1), Input2 (IN2), and Enable1 (EN1) for Motor1 as well as Input3, Input4, and Enable2 for Motor2.

Given that we will be managing one motor in this instance, we will attach the Arduino to IN1 (pin 5), IN2 (pin 7), and Enable1 (pin 6) of the L298 IC. Pins 5 and 7 are electronic, i.e., ON or

OFF inputs, while pin 6 needs a pulse-width regulated (PWM) signal to control the electric motor speed.

IN1	IN2	Motor Behavior
		BRAKE
1		FORWARD
	1	BACKWARD
1	1	BRAKE

The table shows the instructions in which the electric motor will transform based on the digital values of IN1 and IN2.Pin IN1 of the IC L298 is connected to pin 8 of Arduino when IN2 is linked pin 9. These two electronic pins of Arduino regulate the direction of the motor. The EN-A pin of IC is attached to the PWM pin 2 of Arduino. This will control the rate of the engine.

To set the value of the Arduino pins 8 and 9, we have to use the digitalWrite() function, and to establish the value of pin 2, we have to use the analogWrite() capacity.

Connection Steps

- ✓ Connect 5V and the ground of the IC to 5V and the ground of Arduino, respectively.

- ✓ Connect the motor to pins 2 and 3 of the IC.

- ✓ Connect the IC's IN1 to pin 8 of Arduino.

- ✓ Attach IN2 of the IC to pin 9 of Arduino.

- ✓ Connect EN1 of IC to pin 2 of Arduino.

- ✓ Connect SENS A pin of IC to the ground.

- ✓ Attach Arduino using the Arduino USB cable and publish the program to Arduino making use of Arduino IDE software application.

- ✓ Provide power to the Arduino board making use of a power supply, battery, or USB cable.

Arduino – Servo Electric Motor

A servo motor is a tiny gadget that has an output shaft. This shaft can be placed in particular angular positions by sending the servo a coded signal. As long as the coded signal feeds on the input line, the servo will preserve the angular placement of the shaft. If the coded signal changes, the lean setting of the shaft changes. In practice, servos are used in radio-controlled aircraft to position control surface areas like the elevators and rudders. They are also used in radio-controlled vehicles, puppets, and robots.

Servos are exceptionally valuable in robotics. The motors are tiny, have built-in control wiring, and are very useful for their dimension. A standard servo such as the Futaba S-148 has 42 oz-in of torque, which is substantial for its size. It also attracts power proportional to the mechanical tons.

A gently packed servo, consequently, does not take in much energy.

The parts of a servo motor are displayed in the following picture. You can see the control circuitry, the electric motor, a collection of gears, and the case. You can also see the three cables that connect to the outside. One is for power (+5 volts), ground, and the white cord is the control cable.

The Work of a Servo Electric Motor

The servo-electric motor has some control circuits and a potentiometer (a variable resistor, also known as the pot) connected to the outcome shaft.

Take note of the above; the pot can be seen on the right side of the circuit board. This pot enables the control wiring to monitor the current angle of the servo motor.

If the shaft is at the correct angle, after which the heater and the generator were turned off, the circuit discovers that the corner is not right; it will change the electric motor until it is at a preferred angle. The resulting shaft of the servo is capable of taking a trip around 180 levels. Typically, it is somewhere in the 210-degree variety; however, it differs depending on the manufacturer. A regular servo is used to control an angular movement of zero to one hundred and eighty degrees. It is mechanically not capable of turning continuously because a mechanical quit has improved to the leading output equipment.

The power put on the electric motor is symmetrical to the range it needs to travel. So, if the shaft needs to transform a significant distance, the electric motor will go for full speed. If it needs to turn just a small amount, the engine will perform at a slower rate. This is called proportional control.

How Do You Communicate the Angle at Which the Servo Turn?

The control cable is used to link the angle. The angle is determined by the duration of a pulse connected to the control cable. This is called pulse-code modulation (PCM).

The servo expects to see a pulse every 20 nanoseconds.

The duration of the pulse will certainly identify how much the electric motor transforms. A 1.5-millisecond pulse, for example, will undoubtedly make the electric motor rest on the ninety-degree location(called the neutral setting). If the vibration is much shorter than 1.5 nanoseconds, then the motor will turn the shaft more detailed to 0 degrees. If the pulse is longer than 1.5 milliseconds, the shaft changes closer to 180 levels.

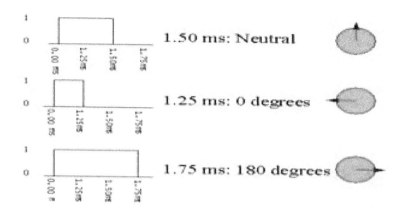

1.50 ms: Neutral

1.25 ms: 0 degrees

1.75 ms: 180 degrees

Requirement

- You will need the following elements:

- One × Arduino UNO board

- One × Servo Motor

- One × ULN2003 driving IC

- One × 10 KΩ Resistor

Procedure

Follow the circuit representation and also make the links as displayed in the photo offered below.

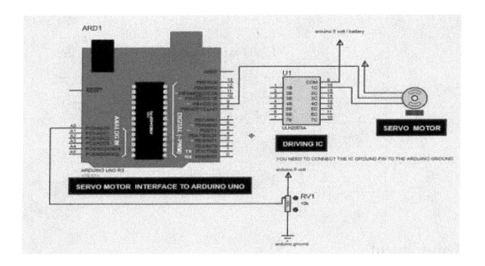

Sketch

Open up the Arduino IDE software program on your computer. Coding in the Arduino language will control your circuit. Open a new sketch data by clicking on "New".

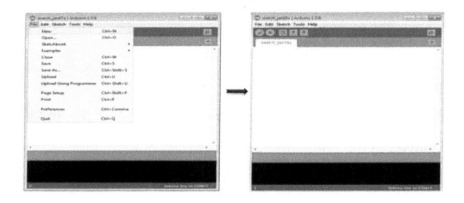

Code to Keep in Mind

Servo motors have three terminals—power, ground, and signal. The power wire is ordinarily red and should be connected to the 5V pin on the Arduino. The ground wire is typically black or brown and should be connected to one terminal ULN2003 IC (10 -16). To secure your Arduino board from damages, you will need some vehicle driver IC. Right, here we have made use of ULN2003 IC to drive the servo motor. The signal pin is yellow or orange and must be connected to the Arduino PIN 9.

Connecting the Potentiometer

A voltage divider or potential divider panel are resistors in a series circuit that scale the resulting voltage to a specific ratio of the input voltage applied. Following is the circuit representation:

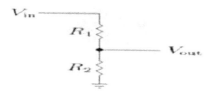

$$ V \_ out = (V \_ in \ times R \_ 2)/ (R \_ 1 + R \_)$$.

Vout is the production power that depends on the used input voltage (Vin) and resistors (R1 andR2) in the collection. It suggests that the existing flow through R1 will likewise flow through R2 without being split. In the above equation, as the value of R2 changes, the Vout is appropriately scaled in relation to the input voltage, Vin.

Generally, a potentiometer is a prospective divider, which can scale the output voltage of the circuit based on the value of the variable resistor, which is making use of the handle.

It has three pins: GND, Signal, and also +5V, as shown in the diagram below:

Result

By changing the pot's NOP placement, the servo motor will change its angle.

Arduino – Stepper Electric Motor

A stepper motor or a step electric motor is a brushless, simultaneous electric motor, which splits a full turning into several actions. Unlike a brushless DC motor, which turns when a deal with DC voltage is related to it, a step motor revolves in distinct action angles.

The stepper motors, for that reason, are produced with steps per change of 12, 24, 72, 144, 180, and200, leading to tipping angles of 30, 15, 5, 2.5, 2, and 1.8 levels per step. The stepper motor can be controlled with or without comments.

Find the Electric Motor on the RC Aircraft

The electric motor rotates very fast in one direction or another. You can differ the speed with the amount of power provided to the engine, yet you cannot tell the propeller to stop at a specific setting.

Currently Envision a Printer

There are lots of moving components inside a printer consisting of motors. One electric motor functions as the paper feed, rotating rollers run the paper as ink is being printed on it. This motor needs to be able to relocate the article at the same range to be able to publish the following line of the message or the next line of a picture.

There is another electric motor connected to a threaded rod that moves the print head to and fro. Again, that threaded pole needs to be moved a precise amount to print one letter after another. This is where the stepper motors have been available.

How a Stepper Electric Motor Works?

A routine DC electric motor rotates based on a direction, whereas a stepper electric motor can rotate in specific increments.

Stepper motors can turn a specific quantity of degrees (or actions) as wanted. This gives you overall control over the engine, enabling you to move it to an exact location and also hold that placement. It does so by powering the coils inside the motor for a short time.

The drawback is that you need to power the electric motor always to keep it in the placement that you prefer.

All you need to know is to move a stepper motor; you tell it to run a particular step in one direction or the other and show it the speed at which to act by following those instructions. There are numerous varieties of stepper electric motors. The techniques defined below can be used to infer how to use various other motors or vehicle engines, which are not discussed in this book. However, it is always recommended that you get in touch with the datasheets and overviews of the specific engines of the models you have.

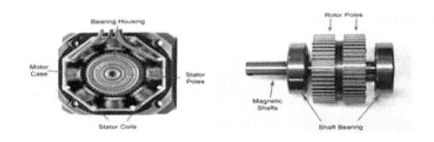

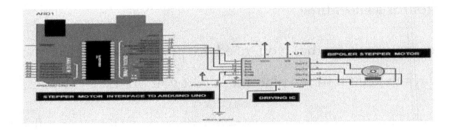

Components Required

You will certainly need the following components:

- One × Arduino UNO board.

- One × little bipolar stepper motor as received the photo offered below.

- One × LM298 driving IC.

Procedure

Comply with the circuit diagram and make the connections, as shown in the photo provided below.

Sketch

Open the Arduino IDE software application on your computer system. Coding in the Arduino language will manage your circuit. Open a brand-new illustration file by clicking "New".

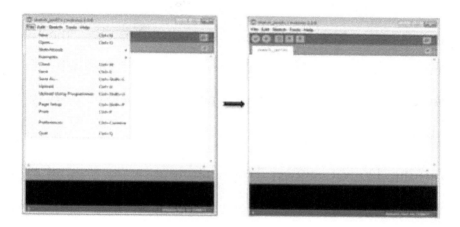

Code to Note

This program drives a unipolar or bipolar stepper motor. The electric motor is committed to digital pins 8–11 of Arduino.

Result

The motor will take one transformation in one direction, then one change in the other instructions.

Arduino – Tone Library

In this area, we will make use of the Arduino Tone collection. It is an Arduino Library, which produces a square-wave of a defined regularity (and 50% duty cycle) on any Arduino pin. A period can additionally be specified; otherwise, the wave continues until the stop() function is called. The nail can be connected to a piezo buzzer or an audio speaker to play the tones.

Warning: Do not connect the pin straight to any kind of audio input. The voltage is considerably higher than the standard line-level voltages and can harm audio card inputs, etc. You can use a voltage divider to bring the energy down.

Parts Required

You will need the following elements:

- One × 8-ohm speaker.

- One × 1k resistor.

- One × Arduino UNO board.

Procedure

Adhere to the circuit layout and make the links as displayed in the image given below.

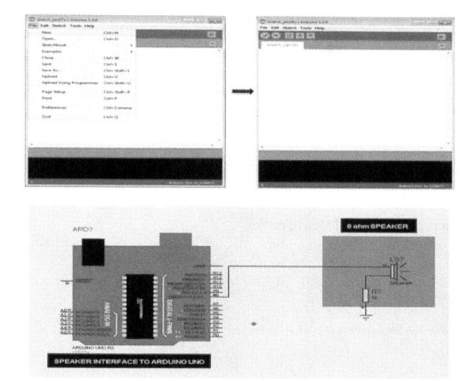

Sketch

Open up the Arduino IDE software on your computer system.

Coding in the Arduino language will manage your circuit.

Open a new illustration Data by clicking "New".

To make the pitches.h documents, either click the switch simply listed below the serial display symbol and also choose "New Tab", or make use of Ctrl+ Shift + N.

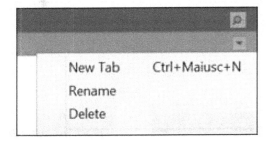

Then paste the following code:

```
/***************************************************

* Public Constants

***************************************************/


#define NOTE_B0 31
```

```
#define NOTE_C1 33

#define NOTE_CS1 35

#define NOTE_D1 37

#define NOTE_DS1 39

#define NOTE_E1 41

#define NOTE_F1 44

#define NOTE_FS1 46

#define NOTE_G1 49

#define NOTE_GS1 52

#define NOTE_A1 55

#define NOTE_AS1 58

#define NOTE_B1 62

#define NOTE_C2 65

#define NOTE_CS2 69

#define NOTE_D2 73

#define NOTE_DS2 78

#define NOTE_E2 82

#define NOTE_F2 87

#define NOTE_FS2 93

#define NOTE_G2 98
```

```
#define NOTE_GS2 104

#define NOTE_A2 110

#define NOTE_AS2 117

#define NOTE_B2 123

#define NOTE_C3 131

#define NOTE_CS3 139

#define NOTE_D3 147

#define NOTE_DS3 156

#define NOTE_E3 165

#define NOTE_F3 175

#define NOTE_FS3 185

#define NOTE_G3 196

#define NOTE_GS3 208

#define NOTE_A3 220

#define NOTE_AS3 233

#define NOTE_B3 247

#define NOTE_C4 262

#define NOTE_CS4 277

#define NOTE_D4 294

#define NOTE_DS4 311
```

```
#define NOTE_E4 330
#define NOTE_F4 349
#define NOTE_FS4 370
#define NOTE_G4 392
#define NOTE_GS4 415
#define NOTE_A4 440
#define NOTE_AS4 466
#define NOTE_B4 494
#define NOTE_C5 523
#define NOTE_CS5 554
#define NOTE_D5 587
#define NOTE_DS5 622
#define NOTE_E5 659
#define NOTE_F5 698
#define NOTE_FS5 740
#define NOTE_G5 784
#define NOTE_GS5 831
#define NOTE_A5 880
#define NOTE_AS5 932
#define NOTE_B5 988
```

```
#define NOTE_C6 1047
#define NOTE_CS6 1109
#define NOTE_D6 1175
#define NOTE_DS6 1245
#define NOTE_E6 1319
#define NOTE_F6 1397
#define NOTE_FS6 1480
#define NOTE_G6 1568
#define NOTE_GS6 1661
#define NOTE_A6 1760
#define NOTE_AS6 1865
#define NOTE_B6 1976
#define NOTE_C7 2093
#define NOTE_CS7 2217
#define NOTE_D7 2349
#define NOTE_DS7 2489
#define NOTE_E7 2637
#define NOTE_F7 2794
#define NOTE_FS7 2960
#define NOTE_G7 3136
```

```
#define NOTE_GS7 3322

#define NOTE_A7 3520

#define NOTE_AS7 3729

#define NOTE_B7 3951

#define NOTE_C8 4186

#define NOTE_CS8 4435

#define NOTE_D8 4699

#define NOTE_DS8 4978
```

Conserve the above-given code as pitches.

Code to Note

The code uses additional documents, pitches.h. This data contains all the pitch values for standard notes. For instance, NOTE_C4 is middle C. NOTE_FS4 is F sharp, etc. This note table was initially written by Brett Hagman, on whose work the tone() command was based. You may locate it useful whenever you intend to make musical notes.

Result

You will certainly listen to musical notes conserved in the pitches.hdata.

Arduino – Wireless Communication

The wireless transmitter and receiver components operate at 315 MHz. They can easily suit a breadboard and work well with microcontrollers to develop an essential wireless information link. With one set of the transmitter and the receiver, the components will communicate information one-way; nonetheless, you would need two pairs (of various regularities) to function as a transmitter/receiver pair.

Note: These modules are unplanned and get a fair quantity of sound. Both the transmitter and receiver operate at usual regularities and do not have IDs.

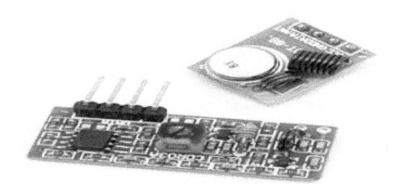

Receiver Component Specifications

- **Item Design** – MX-05V

- **Operating Voltage** – DC5V

- **Quiescent Existing** – 4mA

- **Getting Frequency** – 315Mhz

- **Receiver level of sensitivity** – -105 DB.

- **Dimension** – 30 * 14 * 7mm.

Transmitter Module Requirements

- **Item Version** – MX-FS-03V.

- **Introduce range** – 20-200 meters (various voltage, different results).

- **Operating voltage** – 3.5-12V.

- **Dimensions** – 19 * 19mm.

- **Operating setting** – AM.

- **Transfer price** – 4 KB/S.

- **Transferring power** – 10mW.

- **Transmitting frequency** – 315MHz.

- **An exterior antenna** – 25cm regular multi-core or single-core line.

- **Pin out from left > ideal** – (DATA; VCC; GND).

Components Required

You will need to comply with these elements:

- Two × Arduino UNO board.

- One × Rf wireless transmitter.

- One × Rf link receiver.

Treatment

Follow the circuit diagram and also make the links as received in the picture provided listed below.

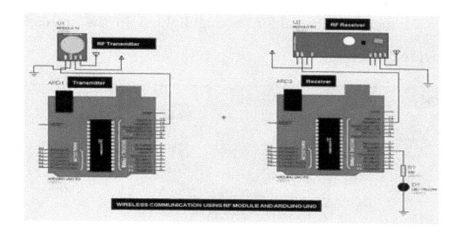

Sketch

Open the Arduino IDE software program on your computer system. Coding in the Arduino language will regulate your circuit. Open up a new illustration data by clicking "New".

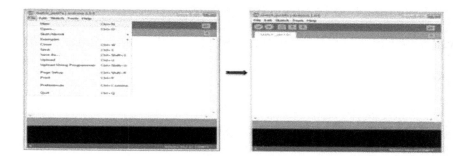

Keep in mind – You have to include the keypad library in your Arduino collection data. Copy and paste the VirtualWire.lib data in the libraries folder, as highlighted in the screenshot provided below.

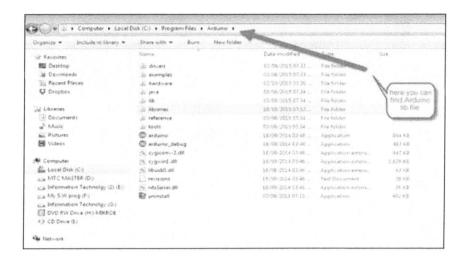

Code to Keep in Mind

The LED attached to PIN 5 on the Arduino board is switched on when personality '1' is gotten and shut off when character '0' is obtained.

Arduino – Network Interaction

The CC3000 Wi-Fi component from Texas Instruments is a little silver bundle, which finally brings user-friendly, affordable Wi-Fi performance to your Arduino jobs.

It uses SPI for communication (not UART!), so you can press information as rapidly as you want or as slow as you want. It has an appropriate interrupt system with an IRQ pin so you can have asynchronous links. It sustains 802.11 b/g, open/WEP/WPA/ WPA2 protection, TKIP and AES. A built-in TCP/IP pile with a "BSD outlet" user interface sustains TCP and also UDP in both the customer and the web server setting.

Parts Required

You will need the following components:

- One × Arduino Uno.

- One × Adafruit CC3000 breakout board.

- One × 5V relay.

- One × Rectifier diode.

- One × LED.

- One × 220 Ohm resistor.

- One × Breadboard, as well as some jumper cables.

For this task, you just need the typical Arduino IDE, the Adafruit's CC3000 collection, and also the CC3000 MDNS library. We are also likely to use aREST library to send commands to the relay using Wi-Fi.

Procedure

Adhere to the circuit representation and make the connections as displayed in the photo given listed below.

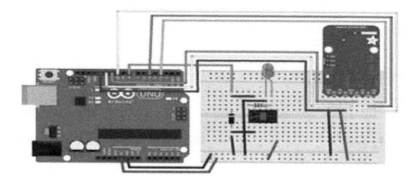

The hardware setup for this job is easy.

- Link the IRQ pin of the CC3000 board to PIN 3 of the Arduino board.

- VBAT to pin 5, and CS to pin 10.

- Connect the SPI pins to Arduino board: MOSI, MISO, and CLK to pins 11, 12, and 13, respectively.

- Vin is attached to Arduino 5V and GND to GND.

Now connect the relay.

After positioning the relay on the breadboard, you can start recognizing the two fundamental parts on your relay: the coil component that commands the relay, and the button component where we will connect the LED.

- First, connect PIN 8 of the Arduino board to one coil pin.

- Connect the other pin to the ground of the Arduino board.

You additionally need to put the rectifier diode (anode linked to the ground pin) over the nails of the coil to shield your circuit when the relay is switching.

- Link the +5V of the Arduino board to the standard pin of the relay's switch.

- Lastly, attach some other pins of the button (usually, the one which is not connected when the relay is off) to the LED in series with the 220 Ohm resistor, and compare the opposite side of the result the ground of the Arduino board.

Checking Individual Elements

You can test the relay with the following sketch:

```
const

{

Serial.begin(9600);

pinMode(relay_pin,OUTPUT);

}


voidloop(){

// Activate relay

digitalWrite(relay_pin, HIGH);

// Wait for 1 second

delay(1000);

// Deactivate relay
```

```
digitalWrite(relay_pin, LOW);

// Wait for 1 second

delay(1000);}
```

Code to Keep in Mind

The code is self-explanatory. You can simply upload it to the board and the relay will switch over states every second, and the LED will undoubtedly turn on and off appropriately.

Adding Wi-Fi Connectivity

Let us now manage the relay wirelessly using the CC3000 Wi-Fi chip. The software application for this task is based on the TCP procedure. Nonetheless, for this task, the Arduino board will be running a little internet server, so we can "pay attention" to commands coming from the computer. We will initially take care of the Arduino illustration, and then we will certainly see just how to compose the server-side code and develop a friendly user interface.

First, the Arduino sketch. The goal here is to connect to your Wi-Fi network, create a web server, see if there is a server inbound TCP connect, and after that, change the state of the relay as necessary.

Vital Parts of the Code

```
#include<Adafruit_CC3000.h>
#include<SPI.h>
#include<CC3000_MDNS.h>
#include<Ethernet.h>
#include<aREST.h>
```

You need to define inside the code what specifies to your arrangement, that is, Wi-Fi name and password, and also the port for TCP interactions (we have made use of 80 below).

```
// WiFi network (change with your settings!)
#define WLAN_SSID "yourNetwork"// cannot be longer than 32 characters!
#define WLAN_PASS "yourPassword"
#define WLAN_SECURITY WLAN_SEC_WPA2 // This can be WLAN_SEC_UNSEC, WLAN_SEC_WEP,
// WLAN_SEC_WPA or WLAN_SEC_WPA2
```

```
// The port to listen for incoming TCP connections
```

#define LISTEN_PORT 80

We can then create the CC3000 instance, web server, and REST circumstances:

// Web server circumstances.

Adafruit_CC3000_Server restServer(LISTEN_PORT);// DNS - responder instance.

MDNSRespondermdns;// Create aREST circumstances.

aREST rest = aREST();.

In the setup() part of the sketch, we can now connect the network to the CC3000 chip:

```
// Server instance
Adafruit_CC3000_ServerrestServer(LISTEN_PORT);//    DNS
responder instance
MDNSRespondermdns;// Create aREST instance
aREST rest =aREST();
```

Exactly how will the computer system recognize where to send out the data? One way would certainly be to run the illustration when the IP address of the CC3000 board is obtained. However, we can do much better, and that is where the CC3000 MDNS collection comes into play. We will assign a set name to our CC3000 board with this library so that we can make a note of this name straight right into the server code.

This is made with the following code:

```
if(!mdns.begin("arduino", cc3000)){
```

```
while(1);

}
```

We additionally require to listen for inbound links.

restServer.begin();.

Next off, we will undoubtedly code the loop() feature of the illustration that will indeed be implemented. We first have to update the DNS server.

DNS.update();.

The server operating on the Arduino board will wait for the incoming links and also deal with the demands.

It is now quite simple to examine the projects using Wi-Fi. Ensure you upgraded the sketch with your very own Wi-Fi name and password and post the illustration to your Arduino board. Open your Arduino IDE serial monitor, and also look for the IP address of your board.

Let us think for the rest right here that it is something like 192.168.1.103.

Then, just most likely to your preferred internet browser, and type:

192.168.1.103/digital/8/1.

You ought to see that your relay immediately activates.

Developing the Relay Interface

We will currently code the user interface of the project. There will be two components below: HTML documents containing the interface and client-side Javascript documents that will take care of the clicks in the interface. The user interface here is based on the aREST.js task, which was made to manage Wi-Fi gadgets from your computer conveniently.

Let us initially the HTML documents, called interface.html. The initial part consists of importing all the needed libraries for the user interface:

```
<head>
<metacharset=utf-8/>
<title> Relay Control </title>
<linkrel="stylesheet"type="text/css"
```

```
href="https://maxcdn.bootstrapcdn.com/bootstrap/3.3.4/css/
bootstrap.min.css">
<linkrel="stylesheet"type="text/css"href="style.css">
<scripttype="text/javascript"
src="https://code.jquery.c the CC3000 chip to om/jquery-
2.1.4.min.js"></script>
<scripttype="text/javascript"
src="https://cdn.rawgit.com/Foliotek/AjaxQ/master/
ajaxq.js"></script>
<scripttype="text/javascript"
```

```
src="https://cdn.rawgit.com/marcoschwartz/aREST.js/master/
aREST.js"></script>
<scripttype="text/javascript"
src="script.js"></script>
</head>
```

Then, we define two switches inside the user interface, one to turn the relay on and the other to turn it off once again.

Relay Control Relay

```
<divclass='container'>
```

241

```html
<h1>Relay Control</h1>
<divclass='row'>
<divclass="col-md-1">Relay</div>
<divclass="col-md-2">
<buttonid='on'class='btnbtn-block btn-success'>On</button>
</div>
<divclass="col-md-2">
<buttonid='off'class='btnbtn-block btn-danger'>On</button>
</div>
</div></div>
```

Client-side Javascript data is needed to take care of the clicks on the switches. We will as well produce a device that we will certainly link to the DNS of our Arduino device. If you changed this in the Arduino code, you would need to change it below.

```
// Create device
var device =newDevice("arduino.local");
// Button

$('#on').click(function(){device.digitalWrite(8,1);});

$('#off').click(function(){device.digitalWrite(8,0);});
```

Finally, if you've found this book helpful in any way, an Amazon review is always welcome!

www.ingramcontent.com/pod-product-compliance
Lightning Source LLC
Chambersburg PA
CBHW071110050326
40690CB00008B/1175